THE TEQUILA LOVER'S
GUIDE TO MEXICO

1998

Wine Patrol Press books by Lance Cutler:

COLD SURVEILLANCE:
THE JAKE LORENZO WINE COLUMNS

MAKING WINE AT HOME THE PROFESSIONAL WAY

THE TEQUILA LOVER'S GUIDE TO MEXICO

THE TEQUILA LOVER'S
GUIDE TO MEXICO

by
Lance Cutler

FIRST WINE PATROL PRESS EDITION, FEBRUARY 1998

Library of Congress Catalogue Card Number: 97-091335
Cutler, Lance. The Tequila Lover's Guide to Mexico/by Lance Cutler.
--First Edition.
p.cm
ISBN 0-9637438-5-6: $16.95 Softcover

Published by:
Wine Patrol Press
17090 Park Ave.
Sonoma, CA 95476 USA

Printed in the United States of America

To my daughter Dawn,
and her chosen sister Lisa,
for driving me to drink,
and thus introducing me to the pleasures of tequila.
Thanks for giving me the high,
and never burdening me with the hangover.

ACKNOWLEDGEMENTS

There is nothing better than friends, except, of course, talented artist friends who generously pitch in on my personal projects.

At the top of the list, thanks to my editor, Lisa Weber. Not only are you easy to work with, but you're a terrific editor.

Bob Johnson, artist extaordinaire, for the cover and the maps.

Dave Ogaz for unraveling the cyber-mysteries that translate my work to the printer.

Michael Parker for his help and printing acumen.

Gerald Asher and Don Yates for their good advice.

Thanks to Gene and Mary Ann Dillahunty for their legal advice.

Rob McNeil, Ann Bringuett, Chris Deardon, Jane Robichaud, and Diego Pulido for showing up at the tastings, and saving my liver for another day.

All the people in the tequila industry who taught me about tequila, especially Bob Denton, Lori Tieszen, Tom Snell, Bill Romo, the Camarenas, and Paul Campos.

Jerry and Catherine Henry for joining us in Mexico to help with the restaurant reviews, thus saving my lithe, athletic figure.

Thanks to Sandy for teaching me about pewter, and for getting on the plane every time I decide to take a trip.

Finally, thanks to the people of Mexico, who set the standard for hospitality.

CONTENTS

FOREWORD

I suppose I owe my affinity for tequila to my father. Years ago, when I was a teenager, my father earned something he had always coveted: a sabbatical leave. As I understood it, if you made it through six years of teaching, you were so worn out emotionally that the school district would give you a year off, at half pay, just to re-charge your emotional batteries.

Teachers who qualified for sabbatical leave were required to update their education, but "education" was broadly defined. My dad's definition involved packing Mom, my two brothers, and me into our 1960 midnight-blue Ford station wagon. He hitched that baby to a used fifteen-foot trailer, and we took off for a tour of the United States.

I got my first look at the Space Needle in Seattle and the glories of the Puget Sound. I sweated through the heat of the Painted Desert and marveled at the Grand Canyon. I discovered the great cities of Chicago, New York, Washington D.C., and New Orleans. I traveled the expanse of corn fields that makes up mid-America, stared in awe at Niagara Falls, drove all the way to the end of the Florida Keys, and strained for a glimpse of Castro's Cuba. For three carefree months, my family and I traveled this mysterious, glorious country known as the United

States. I was sixteen years old, and it made a lasting impression.

When we returned home to California, my parents took my brothers down to Guadalajara, Mexico, where they rented a house for the rest of that sabbatical year. I moved into the trailer, cooked my own meals, did my own laundry, finished high school, and graduated with my classmates. Then I hopped on a plane and flew to Guadalajara. The family met me at the airport. We drove back to the house, and Dad said, "Lance, come into the living room. I'd like to have a little talk."

I'll tell you, he caught me by surprise. I mean, here I was a cocky high school graduate. I'd been living on my own for the past six months. It was too late for the talk about the birds and the bees. What could Dad want to say to me?

I sat down on the couch. Dad walked into the room holding two glasses. He said, "Son, I want you to remember that if you drink alone, it could be a sign that you are an alcoholic." He held up the glasses. "These are margaritas. Your mother won't drink them with me, so you will."

And that's what I did. Every day, around five o'clock, Dad and I would drink a margarita or two. We sat and talked about the events of the day, about philosophy, about life. It was a wonderful thing, spending time with my father, getting to know each other.

My love of tequila is inextricably wound around those memories of sitting, drinking, and talking with my father. Not only were we bonding, father and son, but I saved my dad from becoming an alcoholic.

INTRODUCTION

This book is divided into three sections. Part I: Tequila
Truths and Consequences tells the story of my adven-
tures in Mexico where I was first introduced to blue
agave, the plant from which tequila is made. I learned
how blue agave is grown, harvested, and handled in the
making of tequila. I describe how several different
tequila producers—all very different—ferment, distill,
and age their tequilas.

Part II: The Tastings gives you a method of tasting, describing, and assessing tequilas, loosely modeled
on tasting methods used by serious wine tasters. Using
The Tequila Tasting Form and The Tequila Pyramid™
you will learn to evaluate any tequila and describe what
you are tasting. Chapter 8, Tasting Notes, is a compre-
hensive look at the histories, production methods, and
house style of 28 tequila distilleries. The chapter
includes detailed descriptions and tasting notes made
by a professional tasting panel for 85 tequilas.

In Part III: The Travel Guide, you'll learn how to
visit tequila makers. This section recommends the best
places to stay and the finest places to eat. It tells how to
find the various distilleries and describes the amenities
provided for tourists. Chock-full of tested advice, travel
details, and recommendations, The Travel Guide helps

you plan your own successful tour of the tequila country.

Taken as a whole, *The Tequila Lover's Guide to Mexico* contains all you need to know about tequila tasting and production, and it offers an exciting, adventurous theme for a Mexican vacation. If you like tequila, you will love this book.

As you read this book, be aware that the tequila industry is booming. Fledgling distilleries open every few months. New tequila brands appear almost as quickly as old brands are discarded. Industry changes occur so swiftly that it's virtually impossible to stay current. If you need up-to-date information, log on to these web sites.

www.tequilapyramid.com
www.winepatrol.com
www.mexdesco.com
www.realtequila.com
www.finetequila.com
www.sauza.com
www.mezcal.com
www.cuervo.com

PART I

TEQUILA TRUTHS

AND

CONSEQUENCES

CHAPTER 1

OUR TRIP TO MEXICO

"If I'm going to write a book about tequila, we've got to go to Mexico." At least that's what I tell my wife, Sandy. "We can taste tequilas until our livers wear out. We can drink margaritas until we die of salt poisoning. We can do shots until the acid from the limes eats through our stomachs, but we won't really know about tequila until we go to Mexico and study tequila in its natural environment."

My wife smiles sagely. "If you want to go to Mexico, it's fine with me. I want to get some of these pewter chargers."

"You've already got a gold card and a platinum card," I protest. "What the hell are you going to do with a pewter card?"

She flashes her reprimand look, holding up a magazine. " Chargers, hon," she says pointing to a picture. "You know those platters that go under the actual dinner plates. Don't you think these pewter chargers would look good with our dinner plates?"

We've been married for thirty years. My wife says I make her laugh. I suppose she provides focus.

Pᴀᴄᴋɪɴɢ

Long ago, I learned to physically remove myself when my wife packs for a trip. Two days or two months, it's all the same to my wife. She must try on every single article of her clothing in every single drawer and every closet in the house. Then she sorts the clothes into separate piles according to some mystical grading system. The piles get arranged and rearranged until, one by one, the piles are put back into their respective closets and drawers. The last remaining pile of clothes ends up in her suitcase for the trip.

My packing is quick, efficient, and orderly. Based on a philosophy that assumes a miniscule chance of my returning to any given spot on the globe, and encountering the same people more than once, I pack all my favorite clothes that have worn a little too thin. I pack all those too-bright shirts, the plaid pants, the tight Bermuda shorts, and the old shoes ready to turn over their internal odometers. Sometimes, I even include one of my out-of-style sport coats.

Saved from an ignoble end at Salvation Army, these clothes accompany me to my destination. One by one, I wear them, and then I leave them. As the trip progresses my suitcase gets lighter. I have more room for new purchases. So what if I wear a striped shirt with checked pants? I won't be back in Zapopan any time soon. Who cares if my old jeans are threadbare around the right pocket where I carry my car keys? It's not like the street vendor selling lottery tickets will invite me to dinner to meet the family.

We have one firm travel rule: a single suitcase per person. We each also have a custom-made carry-on bag. These hold our books, music, medicines, and six bottles of wine. One does not live by tequila alone.

TRAVELING

My wife's parents were both native-born Mexicanos. When they moved to the United States, they insisted that their American-born daughter learn only English, no Spanish. As a result, Sandy understands a little Spanish, but she doesn't speak the language at all. It remains a sore point with her. I explain to her that until the 1960s, whole generations of immigrants refused to teach their children their own native languages. They hoped it would ease their kids' assimilation into American culture. My parents did the same thing. I tell her, "I can't speak Polish or Russian."

Of course, my attempts to assuage her language insecurities do no good. When the Hispanic clerk at the airport takes our tickets and sees that we are headed for Mexico, she looks directly at my wife and says, "*Vayan a Guadalajara. Es una ciudad muy bonita.*"

My wife starts a slow burn as I explain, "*Ella no habla Español.*"

"I'm sorry," responds the clerk, "she looks Mexicana." Then to me she adds, "You speak excellent Spanish."

I firmly hold my wife's carry-on bag, in case she tries to club the clerk to death with the wine bottles inside. I abhor violence, and I certainly don't want to lose half of our wine stash. I say a quick "*Gracias,*" grab our tickets, and move us toward the departure gate.

I learned most of my Spanish that summer in

Mexico with my parents. A seven-year stint as a school-teacher in East Los Angeles added to my vocabulary. Twenty years as a winemaker in Sonoma, California, gave me lots of conversational practice. Basically I'm fluent in the present tense. I don't conjugate verbs very well. For that reason, I speak better than I understand. This creates some problems, because Mexicanos assume I know more Spanish than I actually do.

Once we land in Guadalajara, we jump into a cab and head for the hotel. I start speaking with the cab driver, just to practice my Spanish. We talk about the weather. I tell him I'm writing a book about tequila. That warms him up, and he enthusiastically tells me how much he likes tequila. "Be sure to try Pueblo Viejo," he advises. I'm just asking him about baseball and bullfights when we arrive at the hotel. He carries our bags inside. As he leaves he says, "If you go to the bullfights, fill up the baseball stands."

Baffled, I translate for Sandy, who replies, "I think he said, 'You can go to the bullfights, but the baseball team doesn't have a home stand.' " So much for my great linguistic abilities.

We check in at the hotel, toss our bags on the bed, and head for the bar. We suck down a few margaritas, have a light dinner, and then turn in. Tomorrow we begin our tequila adventure.

CHAPTER 2

TEQUILA

The next morning, we head out of Guadalajara on our way to Tequila in a new white Toyota driven by Rodrigo Saracho Barrera, the young local rep for Tequila Sauza. Sandy and I are looking forward to visiting the *fábrica* (factory) where our beloved Hornitos tequila is made.

We leave the city and drive across a dusty volcanic plateau. Wide bands of iridescent blue agave shimmer in the heat, occasionally broken by smaller bands of vibrant green sugar cane fields. The fields stretch out in colorful rectangles. Agaves are planted everywhere, spreading across the wide expanse of plateau to the base of the surrounding hills, and crowding between the road and the low stone walls sur-  rounding private property. Even from the highway, moving at sixty miles per hour, we can see that the fields are well cultivated, with just a few weeds. As we near the town of Tequila, a huge sign proclaims, *"Todo en éste lado es Sauza, y el otro lado también."* (Everything on this side is Sauza, and the other side, too.)

The Sauza tour begins at *Rancho el Indio,* their experimental *campo de agave* (agave field). Luis Arturo

Velazquez Nuñez is the *Jefe de Campo.* Señor Velazquez leads us out into the fields. We stop to examine an individual plant. The leaves of an agave, called *pencas,* look like pointed flat swords. Small, sharp thorns line both sides of each *penca,* which ends in a sharp spike more than two inches long. The agaves grow from the inside out. That is, the center of the plant consists of *pencas,* tightly bound together.

Slowly, one by one, the *pencas* open from the center. The pressure is so great that each *penca* carries an exact pattern of the *penca* before it, like a fossil patterned into a rock.

Señor Velazquez tells us that it takes 8–12 years for a single agave plant to mature. The growing agave is called the *madre,* or mother, and it produces tiny new plants called *hijuelos,* or children, which sprout from its shallow roots. When the agaves are 3–6 years old, the *hijuelos* are harvested. Dug up with a tool called the *barretón*, and trimmed with a *machete corto*, the *hijuelos* are planted in rows to become the next generation of agaves. Each plant produces between 6–10 *hijuelos* per year with about four prime *hijuelos* for planting. Señor Velazquez says, "If the *hijuelos* are harvested too early in the life of the agave, they don't have the strength to produce prime agave plants. If they are harvested too late, they are too tired to produce healthy plants."

He leads us to the experimental fields. "Agaves are normally planted one meter apart in *hilos* (rows) that are three-and-a-half meters apart. Here we are experimenting with double *hilos*. Two rows of agave are planted a meter apart, then separated by three-and-a-half meters where another double row of agaves is planted. This configuration gives us more agaves, but the cultivation is more difficult and costly."

Señor Velazquez introduces us to José Rosario Lopez Reynosa (call me Pepe). Pepe digs up an *hijuelo*, one of the baby plants sprouting from the base of a mature agave plant. He makes a few quick cuts with his *machete corto*, trimming the sides and the top. He harvests three more, and then we follow him to an empty spot of ground where he has run a string to mark a new row. He uses the *talache* (pick) to dig a hole, deposits one of the *hijuelos* in the hole, and covers the roots with dirt. He moves on down the line, and quickly plants the rest of the *hijuelos* in the dusty, volcanic soil.

We follow Pepe to a field of mature agaves. He tells us that harvesters are called *jimadores*, and that they harvest agaves with a *coa de jima,* an incredibly sharp half-moon blade attached to a long handle. He explains that the workers don't wear gloves. Instead, they use grease to prevent blisters and damage to their hands. A file is essential to any worker, because if the blades of the tools aren't sharp, the workers simply can't do their jobs. He hands us his *coa de jima*. It is razor-sharp.

Pepe uses the *coa de jima* to chop the plant off its roots. Then he cuts the *pencas*, leaving less than an inch or two as a stub. Just the slightest pressure with the *coa* against a *penca* severs it. He works his way around the plant chopping the *pencas*. When he's finished, the agave is a rounded ball that resembles a gigantic pineapple, called a *piña*. Each *piña* weighs between 80–120 pounds, and some *piñas* go as high as 170 pounds.

Pepe hands me the *coa*, and says, "Go ahead, harvest an agave."

I take the *coa* and start chopping at the root. It takes a full two minutes to cut through. I start hacking at the *pencas*, using my foot to stop the *piña* from rolling away. "*Cuidado con su dedos,*" laughs Pepe. I'm chopping and hacking at the *pencas*, sweat pouring down my face, thinking, "You better believe I'm going to be careful with my toes." Finally, I work my way around the whole *piña*. Mine doesn't look like a pineapple, or if it does, it's a deformed pineapple with bumps and lumps wreaking havoc on its symmetry. I hand the *coa* back to Pepe who smoothes out my *piña* with a few effortless strokes. According to Pepe, a good *jimador* will harvest 70–90 *piñas* a day. If each one weighs 100 pounds, then a *jimador* harvests between four and five tons a day. They get paid between one and three *centavos* per kilo, so a good *jimador* earns about $15 US per day.

As we stroll to the house, Señor Velazquez explains to us that Sauza plants three thousand agaves per hectare (a hectare is 2.47 acres), and Sauza owns over 80 million agaves. They have purchased additional land in Los Altos, which they began planting in 1997. He shows us a display of the tools used in the growing of agave. Each has a primitive, but functional quality.

Barretón	digs up the *hijuelos*
Machete corto	trims the *hijuelos*
Talache (pick)	makes holes to plant *hijuelos*
Coa de limpia y casanga	trims the agave around the roots
Machete de barbeo	cuts the sides of the agave
Coa de jima	harvests the agave

All five of the Sauza tequilas are displayed at a bar on the patio. The bartender is willing to mix any tequila drink we desire, from margaritas to *sangritas*. When we decline mixed drinks, he disappointedly sets up five glasses for each of us, and we get into some serious tasting. We sample each tequila in turn: the Blanco, the Gold (Sauza Extra), Hornitos, Conmemorativo, and finally, Tres Generaciones. The tequilas are distinctive and different from each other, but share a definitive aroma and flavor. The agave aromas and flavors are moderate, and the tequilas exhibit a wide range of fruit and floral components.

It could be that familiarity breeds prejudice, but Sandy and I prefer the Hornitos to the other tequilas. We ask Rodrigo how Hornitos differs from the other Sauza tequilas.

"Well, Hornitos is our only 100% agave product. It's a Reposado, aged in *tanques de roble* (large oak tanks) for 4–6 months. Of our two Añejos, Conmemorativo is aged in *barricas de roble* (oak barrels) for more than two years, and Tres Generaciones is aged in *barricas* for more than three years." Pepe says with great certainty that Conmemorativo is the finest tequila. Señor Velazquez and Rodrigo insist that Tres Generaciones is smoother and more complex, and therefore a better tequila. Sandy and I hang with Hornitos. "It's got more agave punch to it," explains Sandy.

We shake hands all around, get into Rodrigo's car, and travel a few kilometers to the Sauza *fábrica* named *La Perseverancia*. It's big. Sauza produces 80 thousand liters a day here. The hearty perfume of cooked and fermenting agaves permeates the air for blocks around the *fábrica*. The sweet, heavy air is pierced every few seconds by a screaming, high-pitched whine, somewhere between a chainsaw and nails being run across a blackboard.

We see the mandatory mountain of *piñas*. The *piñas* are relatively small and have very little of the red color associated with well-ripened agaves. The *piñas* are unloaded from trucks and placed on conveyor belts, which take them up an incline and dump them whole into a giant shredder. The shredder quickly and loudly macerates each *piña* and spits the shredded mass onto another conveyor belt that leads to a bank of 20-ton steel pressure cookers

called autoclaves. Rodrigo tells us that shredding the agaves before cooking creates a more even extraction of sugar.

Sauza cooks the agave for 6–8 hours. The cooked agave is milled, mixed with water, and then pumped into large stainless steel fermenting tanks. The liquid, called *aguamiel*, goes into the tanks, where it is mixed with 49% cane sugar. The resulting juice ferments for three to four days, when it has

about 7% alcohol. I taste the juice in one of the fermenting tanks. It is dark brown, with mild agave character, honeyed sweetness in the middle, a strong molasses taste, and a bitter finish.

After fermentation, the juice is sent to 4,000-liter *alambiques de cobra* (copper stills), where a two-hour distillation yields 33% alcohol. The second distillation occurs in 4,000-liter *alambiques de acero inoxidable* (stainless steel stills). This distillation requires nearly three hours with the finished tequila at 55% alcohol.

From there the tequila goes through its various aging regimens. We walk through the plant looking at the bottling line. An impressive room stuffed with large white oak tanks houses our favorite, Hornitos. Rodrigo points out the government seals proclaiming the tequila as 100% blue agave. In the oak aging room, we see that Sauza uses old barrels for its Conmemorativo and Tres Generaciones programs. The tour ends with a viewing of a stunning mural painted by Gabriel Flores. Entitled *El Mito del Descubrimiento de Tequila* (The Myth of the Discovery of Tequila), the mural depicts the ancient production methods, and moves on to a rip-roaring party populated by voluptuous *señoritas* and wiry laborers partying to a marching band. Mystical symbols abound, including the famed *Gallo de Sauza* (Sauza rooster) that appears on the Hornitos label.

The ride back to Guadalajara takes less than an hour. Rodrigo explains that part of his job is to travel around Mexico representing Tequila Sauza. Each town has an annual festival honoring its Patron Saint. Rodrigo goes to these *ferias* and gives out samples of the Sauza products. He tells us, "All the tequila producers go. That way the people can try all the tequilas and decide which ones they like best."

"Sounds just like a wine tasting," comments Sandy.

I tell Rodrigo that we are going to the *feria* in Tepatitlan. "That's a good festival, famous for *mariachi* bands, but the really big one is in Aguascalientes. It is the biggest in all of Mexico."

We discuss tequila and *ferias*, and before we know it, he's dropping us at El Camino Real Hotel. We thank Rodrigo for his hospitality. We spend the afternoon relaxing by one of the hotel pools, sampling a few *antojitos* (appetizers) from the restaurant. We pace ourselves with one or two cold beers, because that night we are scheduled to attend a cocktail party hosted by Jose Cuervo.

THE COCKTAIL PARTY

Sales incentives provide excitement within the liquor distributor sales network. If you are a salesperson who sells the required number of cases of a specified brand, you can earn money, boots, jackets, barbecues, watches, or anything else imaginable. Nothing excites a sales team and boosts performance more than the sales trip incentive.

Tom Snell, as Senior Vice President of Jose Cuervo International, has put together dozens of trips to Mexico as sales incentives to get his distributor sales people to sell Jose Cuervo brand tequila. That Jose Cuervo is the number one tequila brand, worldwide, attests to his abilities as a salesman and a motivator. When I wrote to Tom, telling him about my tequila book, he graciously invited me to attend one of his sales incentive pay-offs. "All of these trips are primarily educational," wrote Tom. "We want to ensure that our customers really do understand tequila and our brand. Hopefully, it will provide a great introduction to the world of tequila."

In the courtyard of the hotel, amidst fountains, ice sculptures, a dazzling array of foods, and three separate bars, Tom played host to eighty people. Sandy and I met Tom, who turned out to be a gentle giant of a man. About 6'4" tall, he sported a good tan, gray hair, and an enthusiasm that made him look fifty instead of sixty. His hearty laugh often rang through the courtyard, cutting through the sound of the *mariachi* band playing near the pool.

Tom explained that he was hosting three separate groups. Twenty people formed the German contingent. Tom said tequila sales were booming in Europe, and Germany was now the number two importer of tequila as a category after the United States. Another twenty people hailed from Minnesota. They seemed quiet and reserved, as if defrosting from their frigid winter conditions, and unable to comprehend this balmy February night in Guadalajara.

The largest group came from Wisconsin, and they had come to party. Big and husky, they were decked out in eye-numbing Hawaiian shirts that barely concealed their bulging bellies, and baggy shorts that revealed stocky, pasty-white legs. They loudly pontificated on all manner of subjects, waving their arms while trailing jet streams of smoke from their always-lit cigars. They sipped margaritas in between toasting each other with shots of various Cuervo tequilas.

Sandy and I wandered through the party, sampling the wonderful food, and sipping a few margaritas. After two hours of increasingly boisterous cocktailing, Tom announced that buses would be leaving the next day promptly at 9 A.M. "Enjoy yourselves tonight, but save something for tomorrow. It will be a long day, full of fine food and good tequila."

The Wisconsin crowd chanted, "Tequila! Tequila! Tequila!" and made dog sounds. "Woof! Woof! Woof!"

"Believe it or not, these Wisconsin guys wear giant wedges of cheese on their heads when they go to football games," I told Sandy. "You gotta love the Cheeseheads."

Led by the Wisconsin group, most of the people boarded waiting buses headed for Nacho's and Charlie's, a rowdy tequila bar with lots of loud music, big drinks, modest food, and plenty of customer participation. Tom invited us to join him and the European contingent at Mr. Bull where we enjoyed a wonderful *carne asada* dinner with lovely Rioja wines from Spain.

We got back to the hotel around 1 A.M., and went to bed eager for the next day.

Sandy told me, "The Cuervo *fábrica* called *La Rojeña* sounds wonderful. I can't wait to see it."

"I can't wait to see the Cheeseheads early in the morning," I replied, "after a full day and night of tequila drinking."

VISITING JOSE CUERVO

The morning featured bright blue skies, a fresh 70° F temperature, and a few hurting revelers from Wisconsin. Bloodshot eyes and pained expressions hinted at their obvious headaches and stomach upsets. Some desperately slurped at cups of coffee, while others sucked down medicinal beers. Sandy and I silently congratulated ourselves on our more conservative evening of entertainment.

When four of the Minnesotans walked in enthusiastically describing the sights during their early-morning three-mile jog, an ugly undercurrent swept through the Cheeseheads. Mumbled threats of lynching were punctuated by whispered slurs about "the health pansies," until Tom announced, "It's time to board the buses. Get ready for a great day."

The ride out to Tequila was subdued, as people talked and dozed fitfully in their seats. Tom told me, "One of our essential goals is to pace this event in a way that ensures people have fun without over-doing it. After all, our primary motivation is to educate our trade customers and expose them to the wonders of the tequila lifestyle. Fortunately, very few of our guests over-indulge."

Nearing Tequila, Tom had the buses pull into an agave field. He passed out straw hats, and the entire group exited the buses and spilled into the field. Tom led us through the dusty fields until we met some *jimadores*. I whispered to Sandy, "Imagine working your ass off for a meager wage, and having eighty gringos in straw hats march across an agave field to watch you. We must make a ridiculous sight."

"I'm sure they've seen this before," said Sandy. "The people on this bus sell Cuervo tequila. If it weren't for them, those *jimadores* wouldn't have jobs. They don't earn a lot of money by United States standards, but for workers in Mexico, they are well paid.

Jobs aren't easy to get in Mexico. Believe me, the *jimadores* are more than happy to put on a show."

I smile, marveling at my wife's uncanny ability to cut to the chase. I gaze out across the fields of agave. The color of blue agave is luminous, somewhere between blue sky and green grass. I know that agave is not a cactus. In fact, agaves are a major genus of the family Agavacae, in the order of Liliacaea, which makes agaves closer to lilies. Basically they look like an aloe plant. All tequila is made from a specific type of agave called blue agave—*Agave Rigidae tequiliana weber, var. azul.* The blue agave is a hardy plant, capable of surviving in some pretty arid places, but it thrives in the volcanic soils of Jalisco.

Tom reminds us that each agave plant needs 8 to 12 years to mature. Mature agaves range from 5–8 feet high and from 7–11 feet in diameter. The *jimadores* demonstrate how to cut down the plants. We watch as they efficiently cut and trim the agaves until the *pencas* lie scattered on the ground like pointed petals from a flower. The regal *piñas* stand like gigantic pineapples.

Tom asks a couple of burly Cheeseheads to try lifting the *piñas*. They manage, but it's a struggle. Tom has the *jimadores* hand their *coas* to a couple of volunteers. He challenges them to race each other to see who can harvest an agave the fastest. They hack and chop, sweat popping out on their faces and necks. I see them straining, relying on strength, instead of letting the *coa* do the work. The crowd is cheering them on, shouting and laughing. Almost simultaneously, they knock down their individual agaves. They start cutting at the *pencas*, when one of the contestants is stabbed by a thorn. He cries out, drops the *coa,* and grabs his elbow. He loses the race, but gamely finishes trimming the agave. When they step back, the two *piñas* are a mess. *Penca* stubs stick out from the core like tufts of hair. The *jimadores* laugh, and effortlessly trim the *piñas* until they are uniformly round.

We return to the buses and cruise into the town of Tequila. *La Rojeña* occupies several square blocks in the center of the town. We line up to enter the facility.

We're handed hard hats, pass through security, and begin our tour. *La Rojeña* is well-groomed, organized, and humming with activity. Magenta bougainvillea decorate the ancient walls with brilliant bursts of color. Mountains of agave *piñas* lie in front of a long bank of *hornos* (ovens). Uniformed workers split the *piñas* and carry them into the *hornos*.

The heavy, sweet scent of cooked agave permeates the air as we file past the *hornos* and enter the sparkling distillation room. Giant polished copper stills glisten against gleaming tile walls, their elegant swan-neck pipes crooked above our heads. The intense, earthy fragrance of tequila saturates the air and creates an intoxicating environment, although I do notice a few of the Cheeseheads turning pale. Tom explains that tequila, like great cognac, is distilled two times. He leads us into the barrel room. Rows of barrels stacked five high fill the cool, darkened room.

Tom answers a few questions, and then guides us out of the plant. We turn in our hard hats and follow him into the dusty streets. We walk a few blocks until Tom approaches a pair of gnarled wooden doors set in a crumbling adobe wall. He pounds on the doors, shouting for them to open. The doors finally swing open to reveal a large courtyard where a Mexican *vaquero* wears a black suit decorated with silver buttons and buckles. His large black sombrero is trimmed with white lace, and he sits astride a magnificent black horse that rears and snorts. In the background a *mariachi* band bursts into song.

The *vaquero* spins a lariat high above his head. He brings the loop down around his body, and then back over his head. "*Amigos,*" he calls, "welcome to Jose Cuervo. We are happy to have you as guests." He widens the loop on his rope, lowering the circle down around his horse, which nimbly jumps through the loop. He tugs on the reins. The horse rears and begins backing up. "Follow me, *amigos*," shouts the *vaquero*, as he leads us into a beautiful garden paradise.

We follow the *vaquero* and the *mariachi* band down a dirt path that meanders through a lush garden. Huge *jacaranda* trees declare their purple-blossomed splendor. All shades of green ferns nestle in the tangled roots of trees. A small burbling stream empties into a large pond. At the end of the path we are greeted by a group of *señoritas* dressed in brightly colored traditional costumes. They lead us across a bridge into a shaded yard.

Ancient trees tower over rows of tables. Two separate tables serve as bars, loaded with the various Jose Cuervo brands of tequila. Tuxedoed bartenders stand ready to mix any imaginable tequila drink. Buckets of ice contain a variety of beers and soft drinks. Somewhere I smell coffee brewing.

A long buffet table groans with more than two dozen Mexicano delicacies, each ladled onto our plates by a costumed matron. Aside from the familiar *tacos*, *chiles rellenos*, and *enchiladas*, we can choose from three different soups, *carne asada* (grilled steak), chicken in a variety of sauces, *lengua* (tongue), *chicharrones* (fried pork rinds), *ceviche* (marinated fish), stuffed squash flowers, three different bean dishes, and several types of rice. Two ladies prepare fresh corn tortillas by hand, molding them from a pile of *masa*, flipping them on a *comal* (griddle) to cook, and then tossing them steaming on our plates.

The variety of food is simply overwhelming.

Sandy and I sip on a tequila and Squirt while we peruse the food tables deciding which delicacies to try. We watch most of the German contingent stick to the familiar *tacos* and *enchiladas*. The group from Minnesota also chooses the familiar items, but they ask questions and tentatively choose one or two more exotic items.

The Cheeseheads' attitude can be summed up in a phrase—"Load 'em up!"

They emerge from the buffet lines with plates piled high, entrées swimming in various sauces. At the tables they eagerly attack the food, washing it all down with a combination of margaritas and cold beer.

Halfway through the luncheon, Tom gets up on the stage in front of the tables to announce that he's arranged a bit of entertainment. For the next three hours, we are treated to *mariachi* bands and marvelous *Ballet Folklorico*—classic Mexicano folk dances by young men and women in rainbow-colored traditional dress. There are machete-wielding jugglers and operatic *señoritas* singing weepy Mexicano ballads. Costumed tenors blast through churning Mexicano folksongs called *corridos*.

By the time the Jose Cuervo Band launches into a rousing version of "Jose Cuervo Is a Friend of Mine," the idyllic afternoon has turned into a rip-roaring party. Waiters swarm around the tables carrying trays of tequila slammers—shot glasses filled with tequila and 7-Up. The waiters cover the top of the glass, slam the glass on the table three times, shouting, "*Uno, dos, tres!*" and then they expect you to chug the foaming frothy liquid.

Tequila is not like other distilled beverages, and

getting drunk on tequila is not like getting drunk on other spirits. Drinking tequila is the cocktailing equivalent of Russian Roulette. Sometimes you can drink lots of tequila and it doesn't bother you. Other times, everything will be going along just fine, and the next thing you know you're unconscious. Drinking slammers is like playing Russian Roulette with only one empty chamber.

The slammers have thrown the party into overdrive. Each new tray is greeted with shouts and chants. The German contingent shares a tray of slammers and happily sings along with the band. One lady tells me that it's just like the beer gardens at home. The Minnesotans have finally thawed. They alternate slammers and beers, and hover around the Cheeseheads. The Cheeseheads have turned drinking into a contest. Tray after tray of slammers are served to the group, where three men gamely match each other shot for shot.

The music pounds through the cigar smoke that fills the garden. Shouts and yells and singing and laughter ring into the dusk. Finally, even the Cheeseheads can drink no more. The wan-looking champion rises from his chair on wobbly legs. With glazed eyes he raises his fists into the air, and then falls over backwards into the ferns. Laughing, the others lift him and carry him to the bus.

As we leave, all the servers, waiters, and performers stand together like a reception line at a wedding. We shake hands with each person and thank them individually for their kindness. The ride back to Guadalajara passes quickly, as we bathe in the warm glow of hospitality lavished on us by Jose Cuervo.

SHOPPING

Sandy and I spend the weekend in Tlaquepaque, the artisan suburb of Guadalajara. Famous for its hand-blown glass, Tlaquepaque has scores of tacky tourist shops interspersed with stores selling gorgeous, high-quality Mexicano crafts and art. Sandy managed to find a factory outlet for pewter. She bought a lot of it. Pewter is heavy. I complain that carrying her purchases has stretched my arms so much that my knuckles are scraped.

"Those pewter chargers will look great on our table when we get home," she says. "That reminds me, we need to get some tablecloths."

My wife has no sense of humor when it comes to shopping.

TERROR TO HERRADURA

On Monday, Guillermo (call me Bill) Romo, the general manager of Herradura, picks us up in a brand new, smoke-grey Mercedes. We head west out of Guadalajara past the Plaza del Sol shopping area and through a large, dusty commercial area dominated by small factories spewing pollution into the air. The streets are jammed with heavy traffic jockeying for position around the traffic circles.

Bill floors the new Mercedes, flies across three lanes of traffic, slams on the brakes just in time to avoid hitting two bicyclists, and explains, "We have a saying at Herradura. 'Think seven times before change.' We make sure changes improve quality. Quality must be in every step. This is the Herradura philosophy."

Bill darts out from behind a truck, accelerates

wildly, and then ducks in behind yet another truck as we narrowly miss hitting an oncoming bus. He talks about growth in Guadalajara's business community. He tells us about the Herradura marketing history in the United States. He talks about the effects of NAFTA on relations between Mexico and the United States. It's clear that he is accustomed to people listening to what he has to say. We don't say much; we are made mute by his driving.

Amatitan, the home of Herradura's distillery, is a small town about six miles south from the town of Tequila. According to Bill it is also the local center for marijuana growth and sales, which he obviously finds loathsome. "These drugs are a nasty business, and the men who run the drug business are violent. Several men in Amatitan have been murdered by these criminals. Now we must have armed guards at the factory to protect our workers."

We turn off the main highway, bump down a cobblestone road and head directly to a small office building. We follow Bill inside where three women in white lab coats work at computer terminals, while he explains to us that Herradura owns four thousand *hectares* with more than eight million agave plants. Herradura keeps detailed computer records on each individual agave plant, including planting dates, field maintenance, harvest dates, and yield.

He leads us outside where we walk about 100 yards down the street and enter one of his agave fields. "All of our tequilas are made from 100% blue agave, and all of those agaves are grown on our own private estates. We harvest individually selected agaves so we can be sure that each agave is fully mature. Larger tequila producers must contract with *campesinos* (peasant farmers) to buy their agaves. *Campesinos* don't select ripe agaves, they harvest by row, and the harvested agaves come to the *fábrica* at different levels of ripeness.

"For good agave, you must work the land. You must keep the soil soft and keep the land clear of weeds. That way you keep the sun on the agaves, and there is no competition with weeds or grass. We clear the rows by hand or sometimes by grazing goats in the fields. We use no herbicides. We produce estate-grown agaves with organic methods."

We climb back into the car and drive a few blocks to the Herradura distillery. High metal gates protected by armed, uniformed guards open to let us in. We walk into a small office and are asked to sign in. We can't help but notice that the entire estate is perfectly manicured, and that the distillery is state-of-the-art, spotless, and incredibly modern.

Bill explains that Herradura employs more than 700 workers. He takes us to the company chapel where Herradura's own priest presides over services, performs weddings, and attends to the spiritual needs of the workers.

We walk over to the *hornos*. "Here you see the workers splitting agaves and stacking them by hand in the *hornos*. The agaves must be stacked properly so steam can pass through for even cooking. Other producers often cheat by using sulfuric acid in the steam to break down the agave fibers more quickly. Here at Herradura we bake the agaves for 24 hours at controlled temperatures."

He shows us two brand-new, modern boilers. "It is important that the temperatures used in cooking the agaves don't fluctuate. Steam from these boilers is injected into the bottom of the *hornos*. The slow cooking caused by the steam softens the fibers and converts

the natural starches into fructose and levulose. No sucrose is produced. We then allow the cooked agaves to cool for 12 hours. This keeps the agaves soft and prevents the sugars from caramelizing.

"Because Herradura uses only the ripest of agaves, the cooked agave comes out of the *hornos* about 26–27% sugar. From there the agave goes to the milling station where it is shredded and mixed with water. Producers who do not use 100% agave in their tequila add more water than we do, which reduces agave character. Then they add other sugars before starting their fermentation. Because the sugars they add are sucrose based, and because sucrose is not natural to the agave plant, their tequilas don't taste right.

"The water used is very important." He points across the yard to a large, modern flat-roofed building. "All of our water comes from our own wells and is run through an ionization system to purify it before we use it. This ionized water is also used for our daily wash downs. Everything must be kept clean to prevent microbes and bacteria from forming."

We watch extracted juice, now called *aguamiel*, drain to a stainless steel sump. From there, the juice is pumped to stainless steel tanks through stainless steel pipes. The entire milling station and the adjoining fermenting tanks are housed under one large roof to help keep things clean and cool. The smell of roasted agave hangs trapped under the roof. It permeates the senses with the heavy intoxicating promise of what is to come.

We walk past the fermentation tanks as Bill explains, "The *aguamiel* ferments between 90–100° F. We only use native yeast generated from our agaves in our own lab to carry out the fermentation. Fermentation runs about four days and the finished alcohol ends up at about 4.5%."

We walk into a spotless distillation chamber with a glistening row of stainless steel stills lined up like sparkling silver soldiers. Immaculate tile floors and walls offset the gleaming metal. "The unfiltered juice goes into the first 3,000-liter still and comes out about 23% alcohol. The second distillation takes place in 2,500-liter stills and produces 46% alcohol. Different stills are used so that no residue

from the first distillation influences the second distillation. The total distillation process takes about nine hours. Taking our time with the distillation allows us to use the prime heart of the distillate."

Bill takes us through the ultra-modern bottling plant. He shows us his twenty-four thousand used barrels from Kentucky. He says that batches of tequila are removed from the barrels and blended in tanks to even the color. No caramel is added. In fact, according to Bill, Herradura uses no additives at all.

He takes us into a large laboratory where several people in the requisite white lab coats are working. The Herradura lab is a marvel. They have constructed a complete small-scale tequila factory that includes a pair of tiny adobe *hornos,* a *moledor,* 20-gallon fermentation tanks, and a five gallon still. "Here we can test our yeast cultures; study the cooking, fermenting, and distillation processes; and slowly evolve our technique to make better and better tequila."

Bill leads us into a lovely courtyard where we taste the Herradura tequilas and dine on a spectacular lunch prepared by the company chef. The proof is in the bottle. The Herradura tequilas are huge, powerful, and complex. Full of unctuous agave flavors, they sit heavy on the tongue and slide down the throat with oily, delicious flavors. The finish is long and lush, full of sweet agave flavors.

I can tell that Sandy is just as overwhelmed as I am. Herradura is beautiful, historic, immaculate, and state-of-the-art. Bill Romo is an energetic true believer of the highest order. After lunch, he walks us around the estate, showing us spectacular flora and fauna, fountains, even white peacocks. Everything is perfectly kept and clean. Finally, Bill takes us into the pride and joy of Herradura, an immense library collected by his forefathers—one of the most complete collections of first editions to be found in all of Mexico. He talks with pride about the history and contributions made by Herradura and the Romo family. He talks about slow, continued growth for his company in the future.

I offer Sandy $100 to trade seats with me on the ride back to Guadalajara. I just can't face the terror of sitting in the front seat while Bill tries to kill us. Sandy refuses. On the ride back, Bill talks about his vision for Herradura, tequila, and Mexico. He zooms up to slow-moving trucks, brakes with bone-jarring abruptness, whips around the trucks, and then ducks out of the oncoming traffic with ever-diminishing margins of safety.

He drops us at our hotel. We thank him and say good-bye. I resist getting on my knees to kiss the ground. That night Sandy and I go out for a few beers and some tacos.

"It's a damned impressive place," I say. "I give Romo and Herradura full credit for what they do and what they've accomplished. He's sort of the Robert Mondavi of tequila. He's taken a good product and turned it into a great one, and it's all done with class, but there's something under the surface that makes me uncomfortable. I mean, what's with the armed guards, and signing in and out of the place? There's something very patrician about the whole set-up. You know, he's the big *patrón* taking care of the *campesinos*."

"That may be true," Sandy says, "but Herradura works because it is the perfect philosophic expression of Bill Romo and his family. If it's patrician, it's because they *are* patrician. If he acts like the big *patrón*, it's because he is. He employs seven hundred people, for Chrissakes. He makes great tequila in a gorgeous place that reeks of money, because he has the money and the desire to make great tequila in a beautiful setting. He wants to continue and improve upon what his father and grandfather left him. He wants to add his mark to the family legacy."

"You're probably right," I agree. "Romo is sincere, and I'll tell you this: he has a great act, and it's as good as we're ever gonna see in the tequila business."

CHAPTER 3

LOS ALTOS

Having arrived a few hours earlier from Guadalajara, Sandy and I are on the fourth-floor terrace of the Fiesta Real Hotel in Tepatitlan. It's a gentle, balmy night. We overlook the plaza, which is dominated by the awe-inspiring cathedral. The plaza is teeming with thousands of people dressed to the nines in Mexicano fashion. They are here for the *feria*, the famous indescribable *feria de Tepa*.

Sandy and I sip Centinela Blanco tequila mixed with Squirt and lime. It's very refreshing and tastes a lot better than it sounds. Suddenly, explosions rip through our solitude. I'm half out of my chair to get Sandy under the table and out of the line of fire before I realize that the fireworks show has started.

For 20 minutes the spectacular fireworks blister the night. Rickety bamboo towers light up slowly, then spin faster and faster until they scream their high-pitched whistles and burst into a brightly colored tableau of Christ on the Cross, or *la Patrona de Tepa*. Rockets shoot from the church stairs with percussive "whumps" to explode directly overhead in brilliant colored sparks that drift down slowly until they gently pelt our table with debris.

We order another round of drinks. I gaze over the smoke-filled plaza and marvel at this perfect example of religion at the core of Mexicano life. Here on the twelfth day of the fifteen-day *feria de Tepa*, where tens of thousands of people suck down tequila and cold beers by the bucketful, where throngs of people come from miles around to eat and dance and listen to the hundreds of *mariachi* bands, the Church is the home and the sponsor for the celebration. Fireworks strung from the wall of the Cathedral itself flame into a glowing finale that integrates life and religion into the daily Mexicano experience.

The party rages throughout the night. Exhausted, we finally turn in around 2 A.M., only to be blasted awake an hour later by such a dynamic *mariachi* horn section that I check to see if they have somehow crowded into our bathroom. At 5 A.M. sharp, the church bells start ringing. Cannons explode every three seconds for a full five minutes. Nobody, not even Sandy, is going to sleep through that. It occurs to me that the church is saying, "Well, we're glad you had a good time last night, but today is another day. So, come to church, pray, and then get to work, feed your family, and return to the party tonight."

We shower, have a light breakfast, and then hire a cab for the ride to Arandas. Arandas is a classic, dusty, small Mexican pueblo dominated by a large cathedral at the north end of town. The main plaza is located three or four blocks south, and is small by Mexican standards, although it has the requisite church on one corner, and the local *mercado* just beyond the church. Arandas sits at the heart of the Los Altos growing region, 6,000 feet above sea level. It has a population of about forty thousand or one hundred thousand if you include all the *campesinos* living in and around the miles of fields surrounding the town.

The cathedral is modeled after Lourdes Cathedral, and Lourdes is the Sister City of Arandas. Catholics are serious about their churches, especially in Arandas. In a typically *macho* Mexicano way, the people of Arandas decided that their cathedral should have the largest bell in all of Mexico. They worked together as a community to raise the money to pay for such a bell. They sent representatives to a renowned manufacturer of bells and hired him to make their great bell. When the bell was delivered to the cathedral, they discovered that it was too big to fit into the building. They found that even if they adapted the cathedral so the bell would fit, there was no way to structurally support the weight of the bell. So, the great bell of the cathedral of Arandas sits on a modest stand in front of the cathedral. The people of Arandas have the largest bell in all of Mexico. It is a source of some pride, and makes for a great story.

About two miles north of town and a few blocks east of the main highway is the Cazadores Tequila factory. I walk up to the guard standing behind the iron-gated fence. I explain that I am a writer from the United States and that I have an appointment to see Señor Gustavo Melendez. The guard tells me that Señor Melendez is in Guadalajara, and therefore cannot see us.

Fortunately, Señor Melendez has given me the name of the plant manager, so we ask to see him. The guard is so sorry, but the plant manager is out looking at some equipment for the new bottling line, so he is unable to attend to us. Still speaking through the closed iron gate, I tell him that we have come from the United States to see the world-famous Cazadores *fábrica* and that I would appreciate whatever courtesy he could show us. The guard nods, excuses himself, and leaves.

The guard returns five minutes later with a lovely lady who introduces herself as Alicia Adriana Rodriguez Robles. She says she will be happy to be our guide and answer any of our questions. The gate is opened. Smiles all around. We each shake hands with the guard, mumbling, *"Gracias, muy amable,"* and enter the inner sanctum.

Cazadores is a modern, state-of-the-art tequila factory. Señora Rodriguez directs us into the large courtyard where truckloads of *piñas* are piled like small hills. Three laborers are splitting the *piñas* and loading them into a stainless steel autoclave. The autoclave looks like a cross between a rocket ship lying on its side and a stainless steel Oscar Mayer Wienermobile. Giant hatches on each end of the cylinder are open. The

laborers split the *piñas* and hand stack them into the autoclave from floor to ceiling and from one end to the other. Each autoclave holds 27 tons of agave. Our guide points to a second autoclave where workers are closing the hatches. She says, "We cook the *piñas* for 6–12 hours to convert the natural starch to sugar. Then we open the hatches and allow the *piñas* to cool for three hours."

The workers load cooled *piñas* from yet another autoclave onto conveyer belts that lead to the *moledor*, which mills the agaves. At this point water is added to help extract the sugar. Now, the liquid is called *aguamiel*, or honey water. The aroma of cooked agave and the *aguamiel* is heavy and sweet, redolent of rich earth and honey. The pervasive aroma of cooked agave insinuates itself into my very pores. It is a warm, relaxing experience, kind of like a Valium wrap.

The *aguamiel* is pumped to large, open-topped stainless steel tanks. Yeast is added and the *aguamiel* ferments for about eight days. Señora Rodriguez explains that classical music is played during the fermenting process to ease the tequila through this transition. I look at Sandy, who smiles back.

When the fermentation is finished, the juice has an alcohol content of 5–6%, and is in fact a sort of tequila wine. This wine is sent to 3,600-liter stainless steel stills where it is distilled to about 28% alcohol, and then that distillate, called *ordinario,* is sent through a second set of 3,600-liter stills to bring the alcohol up to 55%. The distillation room at Cazadores is stunning. A large, open, two-story room of steel and glass with long rows of matched stainless steel stills shining in the sunlight, it is meticulously clean and a bit sterile. Technicians in white coats take regular readings from the myriad of stills, and walk slowly from one still to another, opening or closing this valve and that.

We leave the distillation room and walk through the courtyard to the barrel storage area. Row after row of barrels sits impressively stacked more than six barrels high. Cazadores makes only tequila Reposado, which must be aged in wood, but not necessarily small barrels. Señora Rodriguez explains that Cazadores nevertheless proudly uses only new oak barrels imported from Louisville, Kentucky. The tequila is aged in these expensive barrels for at least 60 days, and then it is blended, and water is added to bring it down to proof. Finished, bottled tequila sold in the United States is usually 80 proof. In Mexico, most tequilas are sold at 76 proof.

To conclude the tour, Señora Rodriguez shows us the current bottling line, and the new, unfinished bottling line and tasting room. Señora Rodriguez graciously thanks us for coming, thanks us for our attention, asks if we have any other questions, and then gently excuses herself. We walk back through the iron gate and say good-bye to our old friend the guard.

As Sandy and I get back into our cab I say, "Sandy, is something missing here?

"Yeah, we never tasted the tequila."

"*Exactamente*," I reply. "Seems to me they're missing a great opportunity here. Well, let's see what happens at Centinela."

VISITING CENTINELA

In Mexico, shops that sell spirits and liqueurs advertise *vinos y licores*. As we drive back into town, we pass several of these stores whose exterior walls are completely painted with advertisements for Centinela Tequila. "It looks as if Centinela Tequila must own every liquor store in Arandas," I remark.

"I don't think so," Sandy says. "Centinela doesn't own those stores. It's more likely that their sales representatives went to the owners and offered to paint the outside of their building for free. In return for painting the building, Centinela gets to put a little advertising on the wall."

"Well, if Centinela doesn't own all those stores, you can bet most of them are owned by relatives of one kind or another. Look, that store is painted with ads for Tapatio Tequila. The two largest families with the longest history in the tequila business in Arandas are Centinela's Hernandez family and Tapatio's Camarena family. All the other tequila companies like Cazadores are new kids on the block. The real rivalry is between the Camarena and the Hernandez families—between Centinela and Tapatio."

We pull up to the Centinela office, on a street facing the main square. I pay the cab driver and thank him. We walk into the office and explain to the secretary that we have an appointment to see Jaime Antonio Gonzales Torres, the manager and part owner of Centinela. The secretary tells us that Don Jaime is not here. He is at the factory, and cannot help us. I ask to see Leonardo Hernandez, the marketing manager. Leo, she tells us, is conducting meetings, but if we will have a seat, she will see if he can come down. She gets up from her desk, offers us her chair, which happens to be the only one in the room, and goes upstairs. Five minutes later she returns with Leo Hernandez, who welcomes us, shakes hands, and escorts us into his office.

We talk a bit. I explain about the book, and introduce my wife. Then we climb into Leo's car and head out to the Centinela *fábrica*. The *fábrica* sits out in a field about a mile from the main highway, surrounded by an eight-foot adobe wall painted white. We enter through a metal door painted orange. If Cazadores is state-of-the-art, then Centinela is, well, rustic.

Leo introduces us to Chuy, the plant manager. He is a thin, enthusiastic man. He wears rubber boots, has grease-stained pants and shirt, and looks like he's just crawled out from under some broken piece of machinery. This is obviously not a dilettante manager; this is a working man. I take an immediate liking to him.

Chuy shows us around. No autoclaves at Centinela. They use traditional rock ovens called *hornos* to steam-cook the agave. He points to the ancient boiler, which drips grease that matches the stains on his clothes. After the split *piñas* have been hand stacked into the *hornos,* the boiler generates steam that is funneled into them. Chuy tells us they let the agaves cook for 36 hours, and then they cool the agaves for another 36 hours.

We watch cooked agaves go to the *moledor,* where they are milled and mixed with water. From there, the *aguamiel* is pumped to stainless steel tanks where a mixture of wild yeast and bread yeast is added. Centinela makes only 100% blue agave tequila, without any other additives. The *aguamiel* ferments at temperatures somewhere between 85–90° F (about the same as fermenting red wine), for 6–8 days. The fermenting liquid is called *mosto fermentando.* Chuy invites me to dip a finger into the tank to taste the fermenting juice. It tastes very smooth, but watery. It has a definite malt-like character, loaded with that earthy, honeyed agave flavor. There is no bitterness.

We follow Chuy as the *mosto muerte* (the finished *aguamiel*) is pumped to 1,000-liter copper stills, where it is distilled to 25–30% alcohol. The second distillation brings the alcohol to 55%. Centinela's distillation room is tiny, dark, and crowded. Both copper and stainless steel stills of different shapes crowd together in a lop-sided harmony. In the center of the room, moving from one still to another, is Don Jaime. A slightly husky man, Don Jaime wears a light blue guayabera shirt and blue pants. He has the regal bearing of a man who knows what he's doing, and is accustomed to being the boss.

 Chuy introduces us, and immediately defers to Don Jaime. Don Jaime is full of detailed information. As he fills one of the stills, he explains that the air from the still should smell sweet of agave, with no off aromas, which would indicate an unclean still. He puts some of the freshly distilled tequila into a bottle and shakes it. He points to the bubbles that form, explaining that *la perla* is a good indicator that tequila is made from 100% blue agave. He pours some of the tequila into a glass and swirls it, pointing to the legs or *las piernas* that form on the side of the glass. This too, he says, is an indication that tequila is made from 100% blue agave. "Of course," he says with obvious disgust, "many tequila producers now use chemicals to give their tequila *la perla* and to enhance the viscosity in the glass, so maybe these indicators are not so reliable."

I taste the tequila. It is still warm from the distillation, but it explodes with clean agave character, delicately flavored with citrus and floral elements. I pass the glass to Sandy who gives an affirmative nod. I ask Don Jaime about his stills. He is less concerned with whether the still is made of copper or stainless steel than he is with the size of the still. "All of our stills have

1,000-liter capacities. As you know, we must heat up the *aguamiel* to begin the distillation process. Small batches make better tequila, because there is less heating time. Cooler temperatures make for smoother tequila."

Leonardo takes us to a large adobe building. There in the dark, stacked on dirt floors from floor to ceiling, are row after row of barrels. "We buy these barrels used from bourbon makers in Kentucky. All of our tequila is aged in these small barrels. We use no tanks for aging. About 90% of our production is tequila Reposado. Centinela Reposado is aged for six months." He points to a paper strip running across the shortened wooden peg that seals the barrel. "Here is the seal placed by the government agents. You see that it is dated. Our Añejo is aged for almost two years. Then we have our Muy Añejo, which is aged for three years.

"For many years Centinela has been a very small company making just three thousand liters per day. Now we are growing very rapidly. By 1998 we will produce fifteen thousand liters per day."

Leonardo leads us back through the plant. We shake hands and say *adios* to Chuy, Letty the Lab Manager, and to several of the laborers. As we approach the cars, Leonardo says, "Now I'd like to take you to our restaurant where we can have some food and you can taste our tequilas."

Sandy perks up immediately. We follow Leonardo and Don Jaime back to the highway, and less than a mile down the road we pull into La Terraza, a restaurant owned by the primary owner of Centinela Tequila, Jose Hernandez. We sit at a center table, and there is a brief flurry of activity as waiters hurry to get glasses, bottles of tequila, ice, Squirt, and Coca-Cola. The locals, mostly farmers with cowboy hats and boots, watch with bemused silence, occasionally whispering to each other. Chips hit the table with two types of *salsa* and a large bowl of *guacamole*. The *guacamole* is terrific, loaded with chile peppers and roasted pumpkin seeds. *Muy picante!*

Leo asks how we would like our tequila. I ask for four wine glasses if he has them. A murmur passes through the restaurant, but the glasses are brought. I pour a shot of Blanco in the first glass, a shot of Reposado in the second, Añejo in the third, and Tres Años in the fourth. I sip the Blanco. It has good agave character, but finishes harsh, and doesn't have the charm of the tequila that we tasted out of the still. I comment to Leo that this tequila tastes different from what we had at the *fábrica*. Leo assures me that it is the same. Don Jaime pours some, tastes it, and whispers to Leo. Leo nods, the gathered waiters nod, smiles break out. "Don Jaime says you are right; this is Cabrito, our new second label brand. It is not Centinela Blanco." A waiter is sent to the Vinos y Licores next door. A bottle of Centinela is opened and poured. Everyone watches as I sip the tequila. The citrus and floral notes are back. I nod my head, and say, "This is wonderful, very good agave flavors, but with an unusual complexity and delicacy."

I taste the tequilas and share my impressions with

Don Jaime. All have that complex delicacy. The Añejo Tres Años is a lovely monster of a tequila; aged and smooth, with wonderful flavors and aromas of caramel and vanilla, like cream soda. Sandy sips the Tres Años, and uses Centinela Blanco mixed with Squirt as a chaser. Leo and Don Jaime drink beer.

Jose Hernandez arrives and is introduced. He motions to the waiters and food arrives. Delicious *albondigas* soup, *empanadas*, and little *tostadas*. As a main course, huge servings of ham hocks baked in an *adobado* sauce prove so delicious that we all happily chew the meat down to the bone. Hours roll by gently. Jokes and humor, lots of laughter, and a warm, relaxing buzz from the tequila. A great afternoon.

When we finally excuse ourselves, the sun is setting. We shake hands all around, thank our hosts, tell them how much we liked the food, the tequila and the hospitality, and Leo takes us to our hotel.

The newest hotel in Arandas is just a mile back into town, on the main drag. A native son went off to Chicago, made his fortune, and returned home to construct this amazing hotel, *El Castillo de Cristal*. The hotel is designed like a Moorish castle complete with turrets and an entrance that could pass for a drawbridge. Inside is a nice, open living area and courtyard, surrounded by two stories of rooms.

It's the mirrors that make *El Castillo de Cristal* stand out. Mirrors cover the entire outside of the building. Every square inch of wall, every spike of every turret, even the entrance floor is covered with mirrors. The hotel seems even more outlandish because it sits directly opposite a stately cathedral. In the Far East you'll find the concept of Yin and Yang, of converging harmony. In Mexico, life is a jumble. Old and new. Modern and ancient. Regal and appalling. It all sits side by side, sharing the same dusty air.

The rooms inside *El Castillo* are medium-sized, clean, and new. I have the sense that the rickety furniture won't age well. The rooms are decorated with mirrors. You can watch yourself brush your teeth, take a shower, use the toilet, or watch yourself watch television. The pretty patio amplifies every sound. We never would have been able to fall asleep if we hadn't been drinking tequila all afternoon.

Ancient El Tesoro

The next morning Sandy and I walk a couple of blocks to the plaza. On the corner of Alvaro Obregón and Plaza Principal is the Restaurant Penita, a good place for breakfast and the best coffee in town. It is also the restaurant where you are most likely to meet Javier López Orosco, the proprietor of Arandas's newest tequila, El Charro. Likable Javier somehow maintains the good will of Tapatio's Camarena family and the Hernandez family from Centinela.

Javier explains why El Charro produces only tequila Reposado. "For the past several years, the young, educated Mexicano middle class has been enamored of brandy and other brown spirits. The horrible crash of the Mexican stock market in 1995 really shook things up, especially within the Mexicano middle class who bear the brunt of economic bad news. They have since abandoned the more expensive brandy and have returned to tequila with a vengeance. Tequila sales within Mexico are booming, and what they are drinking is tequila Reposado.

"It's amazing, in the last few years every tequila maker has come up with a new, more inexpensive Reposado. Centinela has Cabrito, Herradura has El Jimador, El Tesoro has Tapatio."

I ask, " How can they sell it so much cheaper than their regular Reposado?"

"It's all in the aging," says Javier. "Aging tequila costs money. The longer you age it, the more it costs. These new Reposados are aged the minimum, 60 days. Then they're out on the market bringing in money. The other, main brand Reposados are usually aged for twelve months. They have to be more expensive. These new tequila drinkers don't think the additional aging is worth the extra money."

We talk for a while, set up a tour of the El Charro tequila facility for my next visit, and gladly accept a bottle of his tequila.

We are headed for Tapatio, owned by the other grand old tequila family of Arandas. Tapatio sells in the United States under the name of El Tesoro, the Treasure. We are supposed to meet Don Felipe Camarena and his son Carlos at their family restaurant just two doors down from Restaurant Penita, but Sandy advises that we return to the hotel and stash the bottle of El Charro. "It would be impolite to arrive at the Camarenas carrying a rival's tequila."

We return to meet Don Felipe, and I realize that Restaurant Penita, the Camarena's restaurant, and the Centinela offices are all on the same block. To make the situation even more compact, I later find that the offices for Tapatio are directly across the street from Restaurant Penita.

Don Felipe huddles over a cup of coffee, chatting with his son, Carlos, when we enter. He rises to greet us warmly. He offers breakfast, which we decline, but to be polite we accept coffee. Don Felipe appears to be in his sixties. Dressed in slacks and a guayabera shirt, he has an ever-present cigarette in his hand. We talk about the weather, my impressions of Arandas, and the *fábricas* that we've visited.

Don Felipe listens quietly, and then starts his spiel. "Tapatio is the name of our tequila, but in the United States my friend Robert Denton sells it as El Tesoro. All  of the agaves used for my tequila come from our own property. We have close to three million agaves. At an altitude above 7,000 feet, we plant five thousand agaves to the hectare. We use no herbicides. When we clear weeds, we do it by hand. In harvest years, we do no row maintenance. It takes us two to three years to harvest a field. Because harvest sugar is very important when you make 100% tequila, we must select only the ripe agaves. When we have finished harvesting a field, I will not plant agave in that field for at least three years. Instead I plant corn or some other crop. In that way the land can rest and nourish itself for the next crop of agaves.

"Come with Carlos and me. We will take you to *La Alteña*, our factory. I think you will find it a bit different from your previous experience."

We walk around the corner and struggle into a

beat-up Volkswagen van. We head south for three miles and then turn west onto a bumpy dirt road. We drive along, bouncing wildly in the van, breathing in oil fumes from the tired engine. Carlos, who speaks Spanish so rapidly that I have a hard time keeping up, explains, "We cook our agaves in the *hornos* very slowly for 48 hours. Then we cool them for another 24 hours. This slow cooking keeps the fibers of the agave soft and stops them from caramelizing, which can create bitter flavors. Because we use only ripe agave, the *aguamiel* is always very sweet.

"We have a wonderful well at *La Alteña*. Water is one of the keys to making good tequila. We use water from our well to help extract the sugars from the cooked agaves.

"Many years ago we had two plants, *La Alteña* and another one back near Arandas. Tequila from *La Alteña* was preferred because of the water."

Carlos turns up a steep, deeply rutted road, and pulls to a stop. We have arrived at *La Alteña*. Don Felipe explains that *La Alteña* is undergoing some construction. That is an understatement. Dozens upon dozens of laborers work on a giant, multi-leveled three-story stone and cement structure. Huge cement tanks are situated below and to our right. Don Felipe explains that they will eventually be lined and furnished with aerators for mixing the *aquamiel*. A new room for distillation will be constructed to our left. We walk over planks and down a gully to the bottom of a large supporting stone wall. Don Felipe pulls a plug from the wall, and water spurts in an arc into a drain. He picks up a nearby tin can, fills it with water, and hands it to me. "This is the water that flows from the Tapatio birthplace, *nacimiento Tapatio.* It is pure and fresh, and has a wonderful flavor." I taste from the can. The water is cool, sweet, and delicious.

We follow Don Felipe and Carlos around a corner. "This is the old part of the factory. We still make tequila the ancient way. We apologize for the mess, but the construction . . ."

Sandy and I are dumbfounded. If Cazadores is state-of-the-art, and Centinela is rustic, Tapatio is quin-

tessentially prehistoric. Cooked agaves are carried by hand to a circular pit. The agaves are crushed by the action of a large stone, called a *tahona,* which is driven in a slow circle by a small tractor. Barefoot laborers wearing shorts shovel the crushed agave into wooden baskets, which other laborers lift onto their

heads and carry through a short labyrinth of compacted dirt trails. They arrive with their loads at open-topped wooden tanks, where they climb short ladders and dump the crushed agave pulp into the tanks. The tanks have water in them, and a man called the *batidor* is inside the tank. As the men dump in the crushed agave pulp, the *batidor* separates the fiber by hand. Periodically, he uses a hydrometer to take sugar readings. When the contents of the tank reach the proper sugar content, the *batidor* climbs out of the tank, dripping the brown, sticky, sweet *aguamiel* juice, climbs into the next tank, and continues his task. He wears only swimming trunks.

Don Felipe tells us, "Tapatio is the only tequila factory that still uses the agave pulp in the fermentation process. It takes 3–5 days to complete the fermentation." He takes us to another tank. "This tank is almost finished. You can see that the fiber has risen to the top and has formed a cap. When the fermentation is finished, we move the *mosto muerto* and the pulp to the still."

He leads us through the labyrinth down to a small room among the wooden tanks. "We have two copper stills. The first still is 460 liters." We watch as the laborers, once again carrying wooden buckets on their heads, approach the still and pour the contents of their buckets through a small porthole in the top of the still. When it is full, a metal plate snaps over the porthole, secured by a wedge of wood pounded in with a sledgehammer. A small copper pipe runs from the bottom of the still. Clear liquid dribbles out of the pipe into a small barrel. "We use both juice and fiber in this first distillation which takes about one hour. The distillate from this still is 18–19% alcohol. We call it *ordinario*." He lets some of the clear liquid dribble into a cup made from the horn of a bull, and hands it to me. The *ordinario* tequila is very fruity and herbal, and a bit murky.

"The second still receives the *ordinario* liquid only, with no pulp," continues Don Felipe. "This still is also copper, but it is only 300 liters. This distillation takes about 90 minutes. During a distillation there are three parts. The *cabezas,* or heads, contain very high

alcohol and toxic aldehydes. They respire off in the beginning stages of the distillation, and are discarded. *El corazón*, the heart, is the prime, middle portion of the distillate. It is the most flavorful, aromatic, and textured. Finally, at the end of the process are the *colas*, the tails, which contain more methanol. We separate the *colas* and recycle them into the next distillation.

"Here at Tapatio we distill to 80–82 proof, about 40% alcohol. Other factories distill to 55% alcohol or 110 proof. Then they add water later to bring it down to 80 proof. Distilling to proof the way we do at Tapatio costs more, but it makes better tequila, because we incorporate a larger percentage of the *corazón*. Since we have only two small stills, our production is tiny, just 1,000 liters per day."

As we get into the van for our ride back to town, I can tell by looking at Sandy that she is as stunned as I am by what we have just seen. It's as if we walked through a portal into another century. If the *tahona* had been pulled by a donkey instead of a tractor, I am sure that a Spaniard from the eighteenth century would have felt right at home in *La Alteña*. Carlos talks on about the construction and the plans for growth, but assures us that they will continue to use this same age-old technique to produce their El Tesoro brand tequila.

Trying to make conversation, I ask Carlos if Arandas has any local art. He says, *"Tequila es la única arte de Los Altos."* (Tequila is the only art from Los Altos.)

I ask Don Felipe how long his family has been in the tequila business. *"Desde siempre"* is his reply. (Forever.) I have a hunch they are telling the truth, even if it is what I want to hear.

We get back into town and Carlos pulls into a prime parking spot. The parking meter has been sawed off its pole. "This is my father's parking space," he says with pride. "We don't ever get tickets."

Carlos and Don Felipe invite us to taste some tequila. We negotiate a light lunch. Carlos grabs a few bottles of tequila and leads the way across the plaza to a little *taqueria* called El Dorado. The specialty at El Dorado is *tacos al carbón*, succulent pieces of spiced pork roasted on a vertical rotisserie, chopped and served with various *salsas* on tortillas the size of silver dollar pancakes. The *tacos* cost one peso each, about 15 cents. Carlos suggests we start with six each, and then order as needed.

Glasses are brought to the table and Don Felipe presides over an impromptu tasting. "All of our tequila is aged in used whiskey barrels from Kentucky. The older the barrel, the smoother the resulting tequila. Sometimes, if tequila is aged in old barrels for too long, it becomes flabby. So, we blend different batches of tequila from barrels of different ages to achieve the best combination. This becomes El Tesoro Añejo."

Carlos pours three different tequilas for each of us, as Don Felipe continues. "We have more than seventy-five hundred barrels stored in a true barrel cellar underneath our offices, just across the plaza. The barrels are emptied and then blended. We leave 25–30 liters of tequila in each barrel to smooth the way for the new tequila coming into the barrel. What we are tasting here is tequila aged in two-year-old barrels, tequila aged in five-year-old barrels, and the most recent blend of our El Tesoro Añejo. All of the tequila has been in barrel for 26 months."

We all taste the various tequilas. The tequila in newer barrels has an earthy, bold agave aroma reminiscent of freshly poured concrete. It is oily on the tongue and mildly sweet, but finishes hot. The tequila from older barrels has the same earthy, agave aromas, but the texture is much fatter in the mouth, almost too fat. It has flavors of agave, smoke, and earth, and finishes so smoothly that it's boring. The blend for the Añejo is terrific. It, too, smells boldly of agave, but also has hints of caramel and smoke. Full and oily in the mouth, it has just the right amount of astringency to keep from turning dull. The flavors are full of agave, earth and smoke, and it finishes with an oily, light sweet taste that lingers forever.

We congratulate Don Felipe out of genuine respect. We finish lunch, and make our way back to the office. There we see the barrel cellar, the bottling line, and the labeling room. Everything is done by hand. Clearly, the aging and bottling equipment at El Tesoro is not much more modern than the production facilities at *La Alteña*.

We thank Don Felipe and Carlos, and take our leave laden with bottles of Tapatio and El Tesoro.

"So, do you think that making tequila in this ancient manner makes for better tequila?" asks Sandy.

"I'm not sure," I answer. "I know that successful winemaking depends in part on a good match between technology and underlying philosophy. I have seen great wines made by wealthy people, who have state-of-the-art facilities, a scientific approach, immaculate vineyards, and elaborate sensory systems. I have also seen terrific wines made by people who have the minimum of equipment, an almost mystical approach to winemaking, and old vineyards that produce tiny amounts of grapes.

"What doesn't work is a production philosophy that is out of sync with the real personality of the management, like when someone tries to make their winery look like a state-of-the-art, scientific, modern chateau, when in fact it isn't. They spend so much time on the facade, that the wines inevitably suffer.

"One thing I'm sure of, the Camarenas aren't putting on a facade. They do things the way they do because they believe it's the best way to make tequila. It could be that they are too damn stubborn for their own good. It seems to me that a little modernization at *La Alteña* could go a long way toward making their work easier without diminishing the quality of their tequila. On the other hand, if they modernize, they could lose the very essence that makes their tequila special."

Sandy considers that, and says, "I like the way you think about this tequila. You look beyond what they show you into what is in their hearts, and it's very clear that the heart of the Mexican beverage industry is tequila."

CHAPTER 4

THE NITTY GRITTY

The next day, Sandy and I take a taxicab to Atotonilco. The ride takes thirty minutes, and goes across a flat, dusty plateau dotted with agave fields. The fields in this Los Altos area are rougher and less manicured than their counterparts near Tequila, and the agaves appear larger.

Approaching Atotonilco, we pass the town dump, with its wispy smoke trailing into the sky from the burning piles of trash, but the rest of the view is spectacular. Below us, the town nestles around the golden domed cathedral. Beyond, smaller towns dot the valley of a long canyon, and clouds dapple the area with shade and sunlight. We descend into Atotonilco winding through fields of agave that cling tenaciously to the mountainsides. Vertical rows of shimmering blue agave climb from the roadside to the top of each mountain.

We direct the cab driver through town to El Campestre Restaurant, where we are to have lunch with Don Enrique López, one of the largest agave growers in Los Altos. We walk into the beautiful covered patio of the restaurant and find Don Enrique waiting for us. In his early 60s, Don Enrique is tall, maybe 6'2". He wears a plaid work shirt, Levis, dusty cowboy boots, and a giant silver belt buckle partially obscured by his hefty beer belly.

We shake hands. He motions for us to sit at the table. "I hope you don't mind, but I've arranged for the chef to prepare some of his specialties." Sandy and I assure him that we would love to sample the chef's specialties. As Don Enrique opens a bottle of El Viejito Blanco, we help ourselves to ice and pour a shot of tequila into our glasses. We toss in a chunk of lime, a pinch of salt, and then we fill our glasses from the pitcher of lemonade. The drinks are terrific and refreshing. We talk with Don Enrique as a first course of crispy *quesadillas* is served. I explain that I am writing a book about tequila, and that I'm interested in learning all I can about blue agave.

"Well," says Don Enrique, "to learn about agaves we must go way back, before Mexico was Mexico. Long before the Spanish came, the land was divided by two major Indian tribes. The lands to the South and the East were ruled primarily by the Mayans, but the lands of the highland plateaus belonged to the Aztecs.

"A plant called *maguey* was the mother bounty to the Aztecs. It grew wild and was plentiful. The plant itself was harvested, roasted over open fires to convert its starch to sugar, and eaten as a main food source. The sap from the *pencas* had medicinal, healing qualities, and could numb the pain of wounds. Overripe *magueyes* would attract worms called *gusanos* that were cooked as delicacies and thought to be aphrodisiacs. When the spikes at the end of the *pencas* were pulled from the plant, long fibers came out and made a servicable needle and thread. And most importantly, when the hearts of the *maguey* were tapped, drained, and left to ferment, it created an alcoholic product the Aztecs called *pulque*. *Pulque* had magical properties, that enabled people to commune with their ancestors and the gods, so only medicine men and chiefs were permitted to partake.

"When the Spanish *conquistadores* made their conquest of Mexico, they saw *pulque* as the only source of alcohol available to them on the new continent. They brought with them the science of distillation, and the distilled *pulque* was called *aguardiente*. As time went on, the Spanish learned that *aguardiente* made from a particular type of *maguey* called the *agave azul* made the best spirit when grown in the highland plateaus around the volcano and town of Tequila, hence the name."

"Doesn't anyone still make tequila from *magueyes* other than blue agave?" Sandy asks.

"It is prohibited by law. All tequila must be made from *agave azul*, and the *agave azul* must come from specifically designated areas. Finally, the *aguamiel* must be distilled two times to be classed as tequila."

"But not all tequilas are made as 100% blue agave tequilas, right?"

"That is correct," answers Don Enrique. "By law, all tequila must be derived from at least 51% *agave azul*. The base for the rest can come from other sugars, usually some form of sugar cane. These are called *mixto* tequilas."

"Why would anyone make *mixto* tequila instead of 100% blue agave?" I ask.

"Ah," says Don Enrique, "now you have asked an

important question. Agave is an expensive resource. It takes a long time, 8–12 years, to grow a mature agave. They require care and cultivation. We must pay to harvest, and because agaves are heavy, shipping is costly as well. Most of the time agave is much more expensive than sugar cane, so it is usually cheaper to make *mixto* tequila."

"Usually? You mean sometimes blue agave is actually cheaper than sugar?"

"Well, not cheaper, but about the same price. After all, agaves are a crop and must adhere to the laws of supply and demand. Right now, for example, tequila is selling like crazy, prices are high, and the supply of agave is adequate. But everyone with land is becoming an agave farmer. In a few years, we will have a glut of agave. The newer farmers will be desperate to sell their agaves, especially since they have been waiting for at least eight years to make their first sale. The distilleries are not generous. They will drive the prices down. You will see, in a few years agave prices will be the same as sugar prices."

I shake my head. "The exact same thing is happening in California with grapes. Demand for wine is at an all-time high. The past few grape harvests have been small. Grapes have become very expensive, and so have the wines. Everyone with even a few acres of land is planting a vineyard."

Don Enrique smiles, "And in a few years, there will be too many grapes. The price will tumble. The small growers will lose their land, and the large growers will buy their vineyards at cheap prices. They will wait for the next shortage, and then they will make more money. Agriculture is agriculture. Agave, corn, grapes, the crop makes no difference. The rules are the same."

Sandy looks directly at Don Enrique. "We have been told you are the largest agave grower in Los Altos."

'Yes," replies Don Enrique. "I understand the rules, and I play the game very well."

By this time, we have finished the *quesadillas*, a series of soft *tacos* made with pork, and *sopas*, flat corn cakes made from *masa* covered with a tangy meat sauce. Now, we are being served *cordoniz*, charcoal-grilled quail that have been marinated in lemon, and served with a *picante* chile sauce. As we dig into the main course, I ask, "I know that you are probably prejudiced, but is it true that the best agaves come from Los Altos?"

"Certainly," laughs Don Enrique. "Los Altos has the best agaves in the world, and I'll tell you why. First of all, we have the best soil. Second, we are at the best altitude. Third, we have the best farmers. Tequila is much lower in elevation, and their soil is nowhere near as rich as ours. Because of their lower elevation, they must deal with *mariposa negra*, the black  butterfly that can kill the plants. They even have to deal with the smog from Guadalajara.

"Growers in Tequila are at the mercy of the giant distillers. They get pressured to produce agaves quickly. They plant them close together, so the agaves don't have room to grow. They harvest by field, instead of by individual agave, so not all of the agaves are fully ripened. They are cheated by the distilleries, and receive low prices. So the farmers must take short cuts. They use weak *hijuelos*, and use fertilizer to make the plants grow faster.

"Tequila is the drink of Mexico. Here in Mexico we are not fast. We are steady. I think the secret to good tequila is to proceed slowly. Grow the agaves slowly. Harvest when they are fully ripened. Take the time and use *hornos* to roast the agaves, instead of rushing them through autoclaves. Ferment the *aguamiel* slowly, and then run the distillation patiently. Age the tequila in used barrels for at least a year. I think that method will produce the best tequila."

"With agaves from Los Altos," laughs Sandy.

"That goes without saying," agrees Don Enrique.

MAKING GREAT TEQUILA

After lunch on our way back to Guadalajara, Sandy comments, "Everyone seems to have a different way of making tequila. Some use *hornos,* others use autoclaves. Some cook the agave for a few hours, others cook it for days. Some places are incredibly modern, while others are practically prehistoric. What makes good tequila?"

"Well, based on what we've tasted this past week, I think the agave is the most important thing. Making good wine requires mature, ripe fruit, so I assume the same is true for tequila. I know we tend to like the 100% agave tequilas better than the *mixtos*."

"They have more agave flavor," agrees Sandy. "It makes sense. The *mixto* tequilas use sugars from sources other than blue agave. That has to dilute the intensity of agave flavor."

Thinking out loud, I say, "Over in Tequila, we saw lots of smaller, unripe *piñas*. They were all white with no red in the *penca* stubs, but since they were adding sugar anyway, it wasn't as critical."

"That's right," says Sandy, "at El Tesoro and Centinela, there was lots of red in the *penca* stubs, and hardly any *piñas* that were all white."

I remember, "Herradura had the ripest *piñas* of all. They had red in the *penca* stubs, and it often intruded into the core of the *piña*. The maturity of the agave has to be the key. When you make 100% blue agave tequila, using perfectly ripened agaves is critical, because it becomes your only source of sugar, and the sugar controls the amount of alcohol. Then, I've got to agree with Don Enrique, slowing down the process is good. *Hornos* have got to be better than autoclaves. The whole idea behind autoclaves is to speed up the cooking process. Most of the people we talked to said that you had to cook the agaves slowly to prevent caramelization. The agaves cook slower in *hornos*. So, if we're trying to make really good tequila, we've got to use *hornos*."

Sandy asks, "What do you think about leaving the agave fiber in with the *aguamiel* during fermentation?"

"Actually, I like that idea. It reminds me of fermenting red wine with the skins. But I think the fibers should be filtered out before distillation. After all, distillation is cooking, and I'm sure some of the pulp sticks to the bottom of the still and burns. It must be a pain to try to clean one of those stills."

Sandy says, "I know if I had a distillery, I'd only use copper stills. First of all copper is much prettier than stainless steel, and secondly, copper is the best conductor of heat. And then, I just like the traditional look of copper stills."

"I like copper too, but I think it's important to use small 1,500 to 2,500-liter stills. The smaller stills help slow down the distillation process, and it's easier to control the temperatures. I also like the idea of distilling to proof."

"That's one part I really didn't understand," Sandy confesses.

"Well, it all relates back to the speed thing. The whole idea of distillation is to make alcohol. While you're making the alcohol, you're concentrating all of the flavors. It's faster to start with *aguamiel* that's higher in sugar, because it will produce more alcohol in the *mosto muerto*. Higher alcohol in the *mosto muerto* will, in turn, produce more alcohol in the first distillation, the *ordinario*. The second distillation will get as high as 110 proof, 55% alcohol. Then they can add water to bring the proof back down to 80, or whatever they want."

"But it doesn't make any sense to extract all those concentrated flavors, and then dilute them with water," says Sandy.

"True," I agree, "but it is faster to produce tequila that way, and water is a lot cheaper than agave. If you distill to proof, you end up between 80–86 proof. You don't need to dilute with water, and I assume you have more concentrated flavors."

"OK," says Sandy. "So to make good tequila, we

need perfectly ripe agaves. We cook them slowly in real *hornos*, and we ferment the *aguamiel* with the pulp in it. We use small copper stills, and we distill to proof. That's it."

"We make only 100% blue agave tequila, and we put our tequila in used whiskey barrels, never new oak barrels."

"Why not use new oak barrels?" asks Sandy. "You use lots of new oak barrels when you make wine."

"New oak barrels have too much tannin and add too much toasty flavor to the tequila." I explain. "The tannin leaves a dry, dusty cardboard flavor in the after-taste, and the toast quickly overpowers the agave flavor. What's the use of aging the tequila, if it no longer tastes like tequila?

"OK," says Sandy, "no new oak barrels for our tequila. You know all this tequila talk is making me hungry. Where are we going for dinner tonight?"

MEZCAL AND BACANORA

I've cut a pretty good deal for our last day in Mexico. Sandy is in Tonala shopping for pottery. I'm meeting her at a designated spot in exactly two hours to help load all the purchases into a taxi. "Don't you leave me standing in the middle of the street with all kinds of packages," she admonishes.

In the meantime, I'm sitting in a funky little bar trying to pull together some notes. The night before, after dinner, we met up with two great characters. Manuel lives in Oaxaca. He makes *mezcal*. His broth-er Marcelo lives in Sonora. He makes *bacanora,* another distilled spirit made from *maguey*. Both Manuel and Marcelo are cousins of the cab driver who brought us back from Atotonilco. When the cab driver heard we were researching a book about tequila, he insisted we meet his cousins, who were visiting family in Guadalajara.

In the United States, *mezcal* is the liquor that often comes with a worm in the bottle. These are the *gusanos* that infest overripe *magueyes*. As far as I'm concerned, any product that comes with a worm is unfit for human consumption. I mean, if you ordered a salad, and it came to you with one of those worms in it, you'd send it back and probably leave the restaurant.

Any time I've been forced to try *mezcal* in the United States, it's been unpleasant. In my experience, *mezcal* tastes like one of two things—gasoline or creosote. When you consider that they warn you the stuff is awful by putting a worm in it, I could never understand why anyone would drink *mezcal*.

Manuel changed all of that. He explained that the *mezcal* available in the United States is made by giant distillers, and bears little resemblance to the real product.

Authentic *mezcal* usually comes from the Mexican state of Oaxaca. *Mezcal* is not made from blue agave. Other *maguey* varieties are used, with the *espadin maguey* being most common, although four or five other types are also used. The plants are grown all over Oaxaca in small family gardens until they are two years old. At that time, the plants are uprooted, the leaves are bound, and the roots are trimmed. The plants bake in the sun for two weeks before they are transplanted to the surrounding hills. Six to seven years later the *magueyes* are harvested and sold to local distillers.

The distillers trim the *magueyes* to form *piñas*, and place the *piñas* in rock-lined pits called *palenques*. The *piñas* are covered with hot rocks that have been heated in wood fires, and the rocks are covered with a layer of *pencas* or fiber from the plant. Woven palm-fiber mats (*petate*) are placed on top, and these are covered with a layer of dirt. The *piñas* bake this way for two or three days, absorbing flavors from the earth and wood smoke. After cooking, the *piñas* are moved to a pit and crushed with a *tahona*. The pulp is moved to 300-gallon wooden vats and mixed with water to make the *aguamiel*. This ferments on natural yeast for eight to ten days. Then the pulp and liquid are moved to tiny 25-gallon stills made of either copper or ceramic. These are heated by wood fire and the liquid is distilled twice to make *mezcal*. *Mezcal* is rarely aged in barrels.

Manual gave me some of his *mezcal* to taste. It was colorless and had smoky, earthy aromas. Soft and oily in the mouth, the flavors were exactly like the aromas—earth and smoke. The aftertaste was delicate and long lasting, and the alcohol warmed my throat all the way to my stomach, but didn't burn my lips like tequila. To my surprise, I liked the *mezcal*, but the smoky flavor was just too overpowering for me. I honestly told Manuel that his was the finest *mezcal* I have ever tasted.

Manuel explained that every village in the state of Oaxaca has its own distillers. The *mezcals* are very distinct, depending on which types of *magueyes* are used, and the various methods of cooking the *piñas*. Each producer makes tiny amounts, and the methods are primitive.

Marcelo laughed, saying that if his brother thinks *mezcal* production in Oaxaca is primitive, he should come to Sonora and see how he makes *bacanora*. *Bacanora* is made from the *yaquiano maguey* that grows wild in the central Sonoran foothills. Because these *magueyes* don't grow in carefully cultivated fields, the hardest part of making *bacanora* is foraging for the *maguey*. The *piñas* are roasted over a mesquite fire. The roasted *piñas* are mashed with the flat ends of axes. The pulp is placed in a pit lined with a plastic tarp. Water is added and another tarp is placed on top. When fermentation is complete, the fermented pulp is carried to a 50-gallon steel drum built into an *adobe* oven. The liquid is heated by mesquite fires. An upside-down aluminum pot is used to seal the top of the drum, making a primitive still. The condensed steam drips through a copper tube into a bucket, and then the liquor is distilled a second time.

For years, making *bacanora* was illegal. It was the moonshine of Mexico. In 1992 production of *bacanora* was legalized, but it remains scarce and hard to find. Marcelo poured a taste for me. Slightly golden, the *bacanora* had a smooth earthy aroma with much less smoky character than *mezcal*. Oily in the mouth, with rich earthy and doughy flavors, it burned all the way down my throat into my stomach. I asked how much alcohol was in *bacanora*. Marcelo laughed, saying, "It's 92 proof. Not some sissy 76 proof like tequila."

As I write that Sandy found the *mezcal* and *bacanora* interesting, but a bit too harsh and rustic, I remember that I've promised to meet her. I arrive at our meeting place, where she sits sipping a tequila and

Squirt surrounded by 20 or 30 paper bags filled with her purchases.

"Looks like you found plenty to like."

"I could always look for something else," she says.

"No thanks," I reply, "I think I'll just sit here and have a drink with you. Then we'll get a cab and head back to the hotel. I get the feeling I'm going to need some extra time to pack."

SELLING TEQUILA

The flight home was uneventful, especially since Sandy failed to notice my white-knuckled grip on the armrests during takeoff. I couldn't imagine how the plane was going to get off the ground carrying all of Sandy's pewter. Once we were airborne, I relaxed. Except for straining my back loading all the purchases into our car in San Francisco, I survived the whole trip intact.

It's always nice to return home, especially when your home is in Sonoma, California. Sandy and I sat on our porch sipping on a delightful bottle of pinot noir as we unpacked. Sandy showed off her purchases, telling me which purchases were gifts for whom. When she pulled six bottles of tequila out of our travel bag, she said, "You know what I don't understand? How can we buy this tequila in Mexico for $10–12 a bottle, when the same stuff sells here for $40? Somebody must be making a hell of a lot of money, and I doubt it's the Mexicano tequila producer."

"I don't think anyone is making a lot of money," I say. "It's more like a lot of people are each making a reasonable amount of money. Most tequilas in this country are sold using a four-tier system: producer, importer, distributor, and retailer.

"The tequila is produced in Mexico and sold to an importer. The importer buys the tequila, pays the shipping from Mexico to the United States, pays the federal taxes, and pays the custom broker's fees. Both the Mexican customs broker and the United States custom broker require fees, but on a truckload of tequila these fees run only about $1 per 12-bottle case. Federal tax is based on proof, which makes the taxes on a case of tequila about $25. Actual shipping costs are probably $1.50 per case."

Sandy calculates, "Well, that's not even $30 a case. How does it get to $40 per bottle?"

"Don't forget, we're working with a four-tier system, and everyone wants their cut of the pie. If the importer pays the tequila producer $120 for the tequila, then his shipping costs and taxes bring the cost to $150 per case. He wants at least 25% profit, so he sells the case for $200.

"The importer sells the tequila to a distributor. The distributor has to pay state tax and shipping from the main warehouse, and he's looking for a 30% markup. That brings the case to $300. Then the distributor sells the case to the local liquor store owner, who has to pay any local tax, and who's looking for his own 33% profit."

"We're up to $450 for a case of tequila that originally cost $120," Sandy exclaims.

"You've got it," I say. "The tragic thing is that the Mexican tequila producer is lucky to get $10 on a bottle of tequila selling in the United States for $40."

Sandy shakes her head. "That's crazy. The producer has to grow the agave, manufacture the tequila, buy the bottles, capsules, and labels, and then ship the tequila to the border. He does all of that for $10 a bottle. That doesn't seem fair. Heck, if you drink a lot of tequila, it almost pays to take a trip to Mexico, buy the tequila there, and then bring it back with you."

"Well," I remark, "that works, unless you count in the price of the pewter."

Sandy tosses a cork at me. "We're out of wine, Pewter Man. How about another bottle?"

BACK HOME

We've settled back into our rural Sonoma life. I get up early each morning to work on the book before I head to the winery. The grape harvest is upon us, and I am pumped up with making wine. If you're a winemaker and the grape harvest doesn't get you excited, then you're in the wrong business.

I get home just in time to take a shower before guests arrive for dinner. Sandy has prepared a multi-course feast. We serve different wines with each course. The food is superb. The wines are great, and you know what?

Those damn pewter chargers look really cool.

PART II

THE TASTINGS

CHAPTER 5

ASSESSING TEQUILA

From the outset, I knew that any definitive book on tequila had to include several rounds of extensive professional tasting. This became the biggest challenge and evolved into one of the great pleasures of writing this book. Not knowing where to begin, I started with the obvious: I needed tequila.

Dozens of fine tequilas are available in the American marketplace, and dozens more in Mexico never cross the border. Premium tequilas available in the United States may provide good value, but they do not come cheap. We eventually tasted close to 100 different tequilas. At an average cost of $25–40 per bottle, I would have needed between $2,500 and $4,000 just to get my samples. I don't have that kind of cash, and if word got out that I was spending $4,000 on tequila, I worried that it would only be a matter of time before the authorities showed up at my doorstep to haul me away.

So, I sat down at the computer and composed a letter, which I sent to all of the individual tequila importers I could find. I explained what I was attempting to do, assured them of my "professional" dedication to the project, promised that I would be describing (and not rating) the tequilas, and basically begged them to send me some free samples.

It worked. Not only were most tequila importers willing to send samples, they offered information and help with setting up visits to the distilleries in Mexico. I met a great many people who gave stories, hidden information, secret gossip, and more than anything else shared their love for tequila and their respect for the people who make it.

Tʜᴇ Tᴀsᴛɪɴɢ Pᴀɴᴇʟ

Once the tequila samples started rolling in, I set out to select my tasting panel. Chris Deardon was the former marketing manager for Seguin Moreau barrels in Napa, California. His company had made several trips to Mexico attempting to convince various tequila producers to use their barrels for aging Añejo tequilas. Chris signed on and led me to Rob McNeil, the wine-maker for Piper Sonoma Sparkling Wine Cellars. Piper Sonoma is owned by Rémy Martin, fine cognac producers from France. In addition to running the sparkling wine production, Rob was also in charge of Rémy Martin's California brandy production.

Rob and Chris introduced me to Ann Bringuett. Ann was the on-site research enologist at Carneros Alambic, Rémy Martin's California production facility. She had extensive experience in making and tasting distilled products. We convinced her that tasting tequila would be fun and challenging.

Jane Robichaud is director of Beringer's experimental wine program. She also heads their sensory evaluation program. Before that, Jane worked with me at Gundlach Bundschu Winery, where I had personally introduced her to the joys of tequila. She eagerly offered to help.

Finally, Diego Pulido agreed to join our panel. Diego is an accomplished chemist from Mexico who worked as the production chief for Two Fingers Tequila for five years. Diego's father, José, helped manage the vineyards at Gundlach Bundschu. For years, José told me about his son, *"El Tequilero."* I found Diego at Gloria Ferrer Champagne Cellars, where he works as a chemist.

I had assembled a formidable tasting panel. First of all, every member had loads of experience in the wine business, where evaluating and describing different aromas and tastes is essential. Rob and Ann gave us the added dimension of distillation know-how. They brought the techniques of tasting spirits, which differ from wine tasting. Diego provided specific expertise about tequila production. He taught us to recognize and identify the unique characteristics of agave, and helped immensely with our descriptive vocabulary. Chris was our barrel expert. Much of the character of any distilled spirit derives from its time in barrel, and the aged tequilas exhibited tremendous influence from the barrels in which they were aged. Jane used her sensory background to help us develop standards and terminology to describe the tequilas we were tasting. I filled out the group as much for my "common man" representation as for my long-time advocacy and experience with tequila.

We held our first tasting session on a warm December afternoon in 1994. We tasted eight different tequilas—some Blancos, Reposados, and Añejos. The panel was impressed with the quality, surprised by the complexity, and astounded by the range of aromas and flavors. We began to realize the enormity of the challenge ahead.

Based on what we knew about tequila production and basic distillation methods, we first assumed that each tequila producer would have a distinctive "house" style. We began our tastings by sampling whole lines of tequila. That is, we tasted all Cuervo products from Blanco to Reposado to Añejo, including tequilas that were 100% agave and others that were 51% agave. Then we tried all of the Sauza line. From there we went through each line in turn, from Herradura to Centinela to El Tesoro and so on.

We found that each producer did have a distinctive house style, but we found it very difficult to reach an agreement on the terminology we were using to describe the various aromas and flavors. Based on the panel's individual tasting notes I compiled a description of each tequila and a description of each house style. After more than six months of regular tasting, and after reviewing the collected tasting notes, we developed a methodology for tasting tequila.

We used nine-ounce wine glasses, into which we poured one-ounce tequila samples. We found it impossible to taste more than six or seven samples at any given session, because the alcohol began to deaden our senses of smell and taste. We checked the color and worked extensively on evaluating aroma. When we tasted, we took tiny sips, and then spit into large paper cups. We rinsed our mouths with water after each sip.

While we had a great time trying to describe the mysterious, familiar, yet unique aromas and flavors of tequila, the professional methodology we employed kept the tastings from becoming anything like the fanciful ideas conjured up by the term "tequila tasting." I was truly impressed by the dedication of my tasting panel. We met once or twice a month at my home for almost two years. Eventually, we tasted close to 100 different tequilas.

CREATING STANDARDS

We realized we had to develop standards for appropriate terminology to describe the various aromas and flavors in tequila. We looked through our tasting notes and selected descriptors that kept recurring like "smoky," "earthy," or "caramel." Jane then created a set of standards for these descriptors. Because alcohol is the main component of any spirit, she added various aromatic substances to vodka, a neutral spirit with no real aroma of its own. For example, she added liquid smoke to vodka and passed the glass around. We decided if that aroma matched our idea of smoky. She literally mixed dirt into vodka to see if that corresponded with our earthy description. Painstakingly, and through many heated discussions, we developed a group of standards, and we settled on a group of descriptors.

I found it fascinating (and frustrating) that when I asked various tequila producers to describe their tequila, they used terms like "smooth, rich, elegant, and complex." Prodding them, I asked them to describe the difference in flavor between a tequila Blanco, a Reposado, and an Añejo. They said, "The Blanco is fresh, new tequila.   The Reposado is aged for six months to a year, so it is smoother.   The Añejo is aged two years, so it is the smoothest." I explained that I was asking them to describe the specific differences in flavor.   They shook their heads and gave me a look that said, "Crazy *gringo*," and then repeated their wood aging regimen. The *tequilero* in Mexico accepts the agave-based flavor of tequila.   He makes no real attempt to describe it.

Each of us on the panel had an equally difficult time learning to describe tequila, but I think for very different reasons. Grapes are one of the most complex fruits on the planet. During the fermentation process that turns grapes to wine, all the various elements found in grapes turn into complex compounds. These compounds lead to all sorts of aromas and flavors. A good zinfandel can smell and taste of raspberry, blackberry, and even pepper. Chardonnays have been described as reminiscent of citrus or apple, with vanilla or buttery flavors. Because we all had extensive wine tasting experience, we expected to easily describe the flavors in tequila.

We discovered that the aromas and flavors of the agave are unique, probably nowhere near as complex as grapes, and therefore much more difficult to describe. For example, strawberries are not complex, although the aroma and flavor of a strawberry is unmistakable. Try to describe the aroma and flavor of a strawberry, without using the word strawberry as a descriptor.

Blue agave presents a similar problem. It is, in

fact, the bold, unique aroma and flavor of the agave that gives tequila its wondrous magical texture. Describing such an ethereal flavor is close to impossible. On one of my trips to Mexico I acquired a chunk of roasted agave, fresh from one of the *hornos*. I carefully wrapped the agave in tin foil and sealed it inside a zip-lock bag. I carried it home, and proudly presented it to my tasting panel. We smelled it, chewed on it, and tasted it. We even squeezed out a little juice and tasted that. It really helped us with our descriptions, once we had sampled the source product.

If it were possible, I would include a tiny piece of roasted agave with each copy of this book to facilitate your understanding of these mysterious aromas and flavors unique to tequila. Even without the agave sample, if you taste enough tequila, over time, the mystery will be revealed. In the meantime, we will provide the best descriptors we can, until you can figure it out for yourself. When it comes to drinking tequila, patience is its own reward.

Describing flavors and smells is very subjective. In trying to develop descriptors, we not only had to use words on which we could all agree, but we had to use words familiar to most people. Again, using wine as an example, gewürztraminer has a unique and distinctive smell and taste. The natural chemical compound that gives gewürztraminer that distinctive taste and smell is linalool, but who has ever smelled linalool? Canned lichee nuts are loaded with linalool, and therefore smell and taste a lot like gewürztraminer, but not many people have tried lichee nuts. So, to use linalool or lichee as descriptors for gewürztraminer may be accurate, but not particularly helpful.

We struggled for months to agree on a descriptor for certain tequilas from the Los Altos region. These tequilas shared an aroma variously described by panel members as "smoky," "earthy," "creamed corn," and "ginseng root." Finally, someone suggested the smell of "wet cement as it's poured from the cement truck." Another contribution was "hot pavement after a summer rain." Those two phrases described the smell exactly. It doesn't mean we think of tequila as cement, nor do we mean to imply some negative connotation. We simply wanted to use a descriptor that was accurate and familiar.

After finally agreeing on a methodology and specific descriptors, we went back and tasted each of the tequilas again. This time, we tasted Blancos with other Blancos, Reposados with other Reposados, and so on. Based on all these tastings, we have produced the following descriptions. It is not our intent to rate tequilas or to say that one is better than another. We hope to provide exacting descriptions so you can find the tequilas that you like, and then use our descriptions to find other tequilas with similar flavors that you will also like.

ORGANIZING YOUR OWN TEQUILA TASTING

If you wish to do some tasting of your own, I'll pass on a few hints. First of all, you will need lots of water to rinse your mouth between samples. Fresh, warm corn tortillas are the only food that seems to help cleanse the palate during an extended tequila tasting. All of our tastings were conducted using standard nine-ounce wine glasses, which helped us to assess the aromas of the various tequilas. Much of the pleasure in drinking a fine tequila derives from the aromas. You don't get much aroma from a shot glass. If you are willing to spend $20–60 on a great tequila, we recommend that you use a glass that lets you to enjoy all the complexities of the aromas.

One final note about tequila. We often hear that spirits do not age in the bottle. That is most likely the case with sealed bottles, but once you open a bottle, and especially after you pour from it, oxygenation begins. The distinctive aromas and flavors of blue agave react rapidly to the presence of oxygen. We found that tequila left in partially-full bottles lost huge amounts of blue agave character in as few as three or four weeks. The specific and delicate agave aromas became harsher, sometimes acquiring hints of the acetone aroma found in nail polish remover, and increasing the burning sensation of alcohol.

For this reason, I advise drinking fine tequilas in a timely fashion, especially when having them straight. If, in spite of your efforts, you end up with several half-empty bottles of tequila in your bar, you can expect to find harsher aromas and less blue agave flavor. I recommend using those tequilas for mixed drinks, where the aromas will be less noticeable.

CHAPTER 6

TASTING TEQUILA

At the end of this chapter you'll find our Tequila Tasting Form. We created nine rating areas: attack, color, agave intensity, agave complexity, aroma, sweetness/mouth feel, flavor, finish, and alcohol.

ATTACK					
INTENSITY	wimpy	light	full	strong	wow!
TACTILE	mellow/soft			pungent/burning	

Put your nose into a glass of tequila. That initial "hit" is what we call the **Attack.** We divide the attack into two parts. First is the overall *intensity*, and the descriptors are self-explanatory. Second is the *tactile* sensation produced by smelling the tequila.

COLOR					
	colorless	pale yellow	yellow	golden	gold/brown

Color takes on importance because it is a great indicator of how the tequila was made and how it was aged. Well-made Blanco tequilas should be colorless.

As tequila spends time in wood, it starts to pick up color from the roasted insides of the barrel or tank. Describing color is pretty straightforward.

AGAVE INTENSITY				
	light	moderate	*macho*	*muy macho*

Since tequila begins with agave, we start there as well. Certain tequilas boldly let you know they come from the agave plant. Those we call *"macho"* or *"muy macho."* Other tequilas are more delicate, or have been reduced to a point where agave character is not the main focal point, and we differentiate those in the section called **Agave intensity**.

AGAVE COMPLEXITY		
	sencillo	*suave*

Agave complexity is either *suave* (complex and full of character) or it is *sencillo* (simple with little agave character).

In the **Aroma** section (on page 86) we try to describe what we smell in tequila. Basically, we are trying to describe the aroma of blue agave and other complex smells that we can identify. These other aromas can come from the soils in which the agave is grown, from the distilling process, or from the wooden barrels used in the aging process. They can also develop from the way the agave is processed or from chemicals added to the tequila. Volatile refers to those elements that rapidly vaporize when exposed to oxygen, leaving behind aromas like sherry, overripe apples, or even acetone. We list the most common aromas, and we rate them on an ascending scale from *none* to *¡ay caramba!*

Remember, the blue agave is a mysterious and unique plant. The ethereal aromas and flavors associated with agave are intensely distinctive, but unlike anything else. At first, you may have difficulty recognizing elements of our various descriptors when tasting tequila. Don't give up. Be patient. Slowly you will recognize these distinct aromas and flavors, and you will discover the glories of agave for yourself.

AROMA	none	slight	moderate	high	¡ay caramba!
Earthy: ginseng/wet cement					
Fruity: lemon/citrus					
Floral: chamomile					
Spicy: white pepper					
Caramel: cream soda					
Smoky: oaky					
Volatile: acetone/overripe apple					
Other:					

You should be familiar with most of the descriptors. You might not know ginseng or chamomile. Ginseng is the aromatic root of an herb. Used medicinally for centuries by the Chinese, ginseng can be found in most Chinese food markets or medicine shops. Chamomile is the dried leaves, flowers, or buds from a plant in the aster family. Most commonly, chamomile is sold in health food stores or grocery markets as tea. You can buy a small amount and smell the herb itself, or brew up a cup of tea to experience its earthy, herbal aromas.

Note that all of the assessment thus far (with the exception of color) has concentrated on aroma. One of the characteristics of any great spirit is that it delivers what it promises. The color and aromas of tequila send messages to your brain and build expectations for flavor. If all the aromatic indications are powerful, intense, and focused, then you expect the flavors to follow suit. If the flavors are also full and intense with a long finish and a complex aftertaste, you are likely to be satisfied. But if the flavors turn out to be light and thin, and the finish is short or numbs your lips, then you are bound to be disappointed.

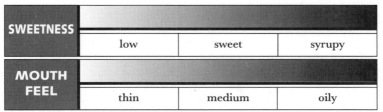

SWEETNESS			
	low	sweet	syrupy
MOUTH FEEL			
	thin	medium	oily

Our assessment of flavor begins with **Sweetness** and **Mouth feel**—how the tequila tastes and feels before you swallow it. We pair these two elements because mouth feel is often influenced by sweetness.

FLAVOR	none	slight	moderate	high	¡ay caramba!
Agave					
Fruit/floral					
Spice/pepper					
Caramel					
Oak					
Smoky					
Acetone/overripe apple					
Other:					

Flavor is the section that deals with the taste of tequila in the mouth and immediately after swallowing. Here we use the same ascending scale from *none* to *¡ay caramba!*

FINISH				
SWEETNESS	none	low	medium	high
BITTERNESS	none	low	medium	high
DURATION OF FLAVOR	short		medium	long
FLAVOR				

Finally, there is the **Finish,** which describes what happens in the mouth after you swallow the tequila. The finish is often different from what happens before you swallow the tequila. Long lasting, pleasant flavors are evidence of a well-distilled, excellent product. In the finish, we rate aftertaste using levels of *bitterness* and *sweetness*.

We rate the length of aftertaste in *duration of flavor*, and if a distinctive *flavor* dominates the aftertaste, we enter it in the blank space.

ALCOHOL			
	tingly	hot	lip numbing

We rate **Alcohol** on an ascending scale from *tingly* to *hot* to *lip numbing,* according to how much it burns.

I would like to point out that tasting tequila in this analytical fashion gave us the ability to describe the differences unique to each tequila, but I do not recommend it as the way to enjoy tequila. I have included several blank Tequila Tasting Forms at the end of this book so you can try your hand at rating different tequilas, but breaking a glass of tequila down into its component parts might reduce your enjoyment of that tequila.

When you drink fine tequila, take the time to look at the tequila in your glass. The color and viscosity hint at what is to come. Put your nose above the rim of the glass and inhale. The wonderful complex aromas that come from distilled blue agave are one of the true pleasures unique to this fantastic product. Finally, sip the tequila. Fine tequilas should be savored for all their rich, complex flavors. Slamming down tequila shots just doesn't allow for a full appreciation of those complexities.

THE TEQUILA TASTING FORM

TEQUILA	
DATE TASTED	NOM

ATTACK					
INTENSITY	wimpy	light	full	strong	wow!
TACTILE	mellow/soft			pungent/burning	

COLOR					
	colorless	pale yellow	yellow	golden	gold/brown

AGAVE COMPLEXITY		
	sencillo	suave

AGAVE INTENSITY				
	light	moderate	macho	muy macho

AROMA	none	slight	moderate	high	¡ay caramba!
Earthy: ginseng/wet cement					
Fruity: lemon/citrus					
Floral: chamomile					
Spicy: white pepper					
Caramel: cream soda					
Smoky: oaky					
Volatile: acetone/overripe apple					
Other:					

SWEETNESS		
low	sweet	syrupy

THE TEQUILA TASTING FORM
SIDE TWO

MOUTH FEEL			
	thin	medium	oily

FLAVOR					
	none	slight	moderate	high	¡ay caramba!
Agave					
Fruit/floral					
Spice/pepper					
Caramel					
Oak					
Smoky					
Acetone/overripe apple					
Other:					

FINISH				
SWEETNESS	none	low	medium	high
BITTERNESS	none	low	medium	high
DURATION OF FLAVOR	short	medium		long
FLAVOR				

ALCOHOL			
	tingly	hot	lip numbing

COMMENTS

THE TEQUILA PYRAMID™

One of the great things about tequila is that it has a personality of its own. Tequila is a drink of the people. Margaritas are boisterous cocktails meant to be consumed with friends in loud places serving plenty of good food. Perhaps because of its common-man Mexicano heritage, tequila resists being serious. Tequila is fun.

I certainly don't want to be known as the man who took the fun out of tequila. You may find the Tequila Tasting Form useful. You may enjoy using it at home to test your skill at recognizing the varied aromas and flavors of different tequilas. But if you are out partying and pounding down margaritas, the last thing you need to do is start "assessing tequila."

If you want to pay some attention to the tequila you are drinking in a rocking, fun-filled situation, you need to use The Tequila Pyramid™. We designed it to be fun, so don't take it too seriously.

THE TEQUILA PYRAMID™

A DESCRIPTIVE TOOL FOR THE TEQUILA AFICIONADO

Using The Tequila Pyramid™ is easy. The four outside steps of the pyramid categorize and then describe Aromas. Across the bottom are five flavors to assess, rated on an ascending scale from *Nada* to *¡Ay Caramba!* We also rate Sweetness and Bitterness on an ascending scale. Coming down the center steps, we rate Alcohol, Duration of Flavor and then give an overall rating.

THE TEQUILA PYRAMID™

A DESCRIPTIVE TOOL FOR THE TEQUILA AFICIONADO

Tequila is a magical spirit made from the blue agave plant. The blue agave takes 8–10 years to mature, and then it is harvested only once. The agave is baked in ovens to convert natural starches into sugars. The cooked agave is milled, mixed with water, and fermented. The fermented liquid is distilled twice to make tequila.

There are two kinds of tequila: those derived and distilled from 100% blue agave, and *mixto* tequilas derived and distilled from a mixture of blue agave and other sugars. Tequila falls into four classes. Blanco or Silver is unaged tequila. Gold or Joven Abocado is unaged tequila with coloring added. Reposado tequila is aged in wood from two months to one year. Añejo tequila spends a minimum of one year in oak barrels.

True enjoyment of tequila requires an appreciation of the unique aromas and flavors derived from the blue agave plant, the distillation methods, and the aging process. **The Tequila Pyramid™** has been developed to facilitate your evaluation of individual tequilas.

Using **The Tequila Pyramid™** is easy. The four outside steps of the pyramid categorize and then describe **Aromas**. The categories are Earth, Oak, Fruit/Floral, and Spice. There are five **Flavors** to assess: Agave, Fruit, Pepper, Oak, and Caramel. Each of these is rated on an ascending scale from *Nada* to *¡Ay Caramba!* We also rate **Sweetness** and **Bitterness** on an ascending scale. Coming down the center stairs of the pyramid, we rate **Alcohol, Duration of flavor**, and then give an overall rating—*malo, bueno*, or *Olé!*

Here's how it works. Evaluating a fine Blanco tequila might yield this description: Earthy ginseng and smoky aromas with hints of citrus, and white pepper. *Macho* agave flavors with moderate fruit and pepper, but *nada* on oak or caramel. Moderately sweet and slightly bitter. The alcohol is lip numbing; the duration of flavor is long. Overall, a *bueno* tequila.

Evaluating a rich Añejo tequila could lead to this description: Intense wet cement, vanilla, and caramel aromas with hints of smoke and white pepper. *Macho* agave with *¡Ay Caramba!* toasty oak and caramel flavors followed by moderate pepper and light fruit. Moderately sweet and moderately bitter with tingly alcohol and a long finish. *Ole!*

Order your favorite tequila and give **The Tequila Pyramid**™ a try. The more you learn about tequila, the better you'll like it.

CHAPTER 7

TEQUILA BASICS

By Mexican law, there are two types of tequila: those made from 100% blue agave sugars, and those made from at least 51% blue agave sugar blended with other sugars. These blended tequilas are called *mixtos* and usually involve the addition of *piloncillo*, a form of dried sugar cane juice. Moreover, by law, blue agaves must come from the Mexican state of Jalisco, or from specifically designated growing areas in Michoacan, Nayarit, Guanajuato, or Tamaulipas

On the other hand, this is Mexico, so the law is not nearly so cut and dried as we might think. On several occasions, distilleries have been shut down by government agents for longer or shorter periods of time, because they were caught using less than 51% blue agave in the distillation process. One legendary bust involved the confiscation of shipments of bulk tequila going to the United States that had 0% blue agave, and had been made instead with chemical agave flavorings.

Important people within the industry, primarily high-end producers of 100% blue agave tequilas and agave farmers, have campaigned for years to force the government to crack down on disreputable producers who fail to comply with regulations. Their main targets have been giant corporate producers, who steadfastly deny the allegations, but who just as steadfastly refuse to give out details of their production and harvest information. Add to the mix the Mexicano cultural preference for telling people what they want to hear, and it becomes next to impossible to obtain definitive information regarding the exact makeup of any tequila. For the purposes of this book, we are going to accept what the individual tequila companies tell us. Therefore, as I began, there are two types of tequila: those made from 100% blue agave, and those made from 51% blue agave. If a tequila uses 100% blue agave in its production, it will say so on the label. If the label doesn't say 100% blue agave, then the tequila in that bottle contains other sugars in the mix.

Although each distillery has its own methodology, tequila production is pretty straightforward. Agaves are harvested and cooked, either in autoclaves or traditional ovens called *hornos,* to convert natural starches into sugars. The cooked agaves are shredded, water is added, and the resulting juice called *aguamiel* is pumped to tanks for fermentation. In the case of 51% tequilas, additional sugars and water are added at this time. After fermentation, the juice is distilled twice. Basically, that's it.

There are four tequila classifications, and they have to do with the way tequila is aged.

- **Blanco** or **Silver** tequila is not aged. It can be stored up to 60 days before bottling.

• **Joven Abocado** is Blanco tequila with
  coloring added to appear aged. This is
  the ubiquitous Gold tequila sold
  everywhere in the United States, but
  rarely seen in Mexico outside of tourist
  venues.
• **Reposado** tequila must be aged from two
  months to one year, in wooden containers
  of any size.
• **Añejo** tequila is aged in oak barrels for a
  minimum of one year.

These four classifications deal only with the aging
of tequila. They are not specific to the two types of
tequila. In other words, an Añejo tequila could be made
from 100% blue agave or it could be a *mixto* made from
51% blue agave. The term Añejo only guarantees that
the tequila was aged in oak barrels for at least a year. It
does not address the percentage of agave used in the
tequila production.

At any given distillery, all four classifications of
tequila usually come from the same source. For example, the agaves for all Herradura tequilas are harvested,
cooked, fermented, and distilled in the same way. The
only difference between Herradura Blanco, Herradura
Reposado, and Herradura Añejo is the amount and
type of aging they receive.

This is true even at the giant distilleries like
Cuervo and Sauza. Cuervo Silver, Cuervo Gold, and
Cuervo 1800 are all *mixto* tequilas produced in basi-
cally the same way. Sauza Blanco, Sauza Gold, and
Sauza Conmemorativo are all *mixtos* produced in
essentially the same way. The only differences are in the

aging process. Recently, consumer demands for 100% blue agave tequilas have convinced Cuervo to produce Tradicional and Reserva de la Familia. Sauza now produces Hornitos, Galardon, and Tres Generaciones as 100% blue agave tequilas.

Because all tequila from any given distillery is usually produced in exactly the same way, house style is the first and most important consideration for the consumer. You can check the NOM (*Norma Oficial Mexicana*) number on the label to determine which distillery is making the tequila you are drinking. Each tequila distillery is given an NOM identity number, and every bottle of tequila produced in Mexico should have an NOM number on its label. Some distilleries produce dozens of different brands, but the tequila is basically the same. All tequilas with the same NOM number come from the same distillery.

Because house style is so important, I have chosen to describe the results of our tastings by producer. Distilleries often make tequila under more than one brand name, so I have also included major secondary labels in the listings. I will give a brief history of each producer, discuss each producer's tequila production methodology, and then list our detailed tasting notes on each tequila produced by that company.

Because taste is so personal, I have deliberately avoided any kind of rating system. One of the joys of drinking tequila is the wide variety of aromas and tastes available to the consumer. However, you should know that I definitely have my preferences. First and foremost, I like my tequilas to taste like agave. My favorite descriptor for agave, especially the agave from the Los Altos region, is "wet cement," which I use to describe that combination of earthy, smoky, fresh-rain-on-the-pavement aroma unique to tequila.

I prefer Blanco tequilas that are full of clean, fresh agave aromas and flavors, but that also have plenty of spice, fruit, and floral components. I allow for Blancos to be a little hotter and harsher than aged tequilas. In Reposados, I look for balance. I am willing to sacrifice some of the freshness of a fine Blanco if I gain smoothness and complexity. Unfortunately, Reposados often lose too much of the fresh Blanco flavors, and remain harsh and hot. Reposados should show hints of caramel aroma and flavor in addition to the spice, fruit and floral components, but they should still be dominated by agave.

I prefer Añejos that proudly assert their agave heritage, and quickly introduce layers of complex pepper, fruit, and floral textures. I love that unique Añejo character of toasty oak and caramel that smells and tastes like rich cream soda—especially when it implies sweetness, but finishes dry. Harsh or lip numbing Añejos make no sense. After all, the whole purpose of aging tequila in the first place is to smooth out the edges, to tame the harshness, and to build body and smoothness.

I have problems with the new long-aged, super-premium, high-priced tequilas that are popping up for every brand, and selling in the $100–250 US price range. Gorgeous bottles and packages adorn these products, but I'm more interested in the tequila. In almost every instance, oak flavors overpower and dominate the agave character. These tequilas often remind me of bourbon. If I want bourbon, I'll buy it. When I want a good aged tequila, I'll stick with my favorite Añejos. At least I can afford most of those.

In spite of my attempt to be as objective as I can in describing the tequilas listed in this book, I'm sure these preferences have colored my notes. There is no reason for you to like the same things I like. Therefore, at the end of this chapter you'll find a table called Tequilas by Style. I hope that you will find tequilas that you like, and then use the table to discover other tequilas with similar flavor profiles that you may also like.

CHAPTER 8

TASTING NOTES

Cazadores
(NOM 1128)

Founded in 1973 by six brothers from the Bañuelos family, Cazadores is one of the biggest success stories in the modern tequila business. This new, ultra-modern distillery opened in 1994 on the outskirts of Arandas. Plans for expansion include a hospitality center, a restaurant, and a new hotel scheduled to open late in 1997.

The Bañuelos family anticipated the recent growth in popularity of Reposado tequilas. With the opening of their new distillery, they introduced a fine *mixto* Reposado. Using autoclaves, stainless steel tanks, and state of the art distillation equipment, they made their tequila quickly, which lowered their production costs. They aged the tequila 70 days in new oak barrels. They touted the quality using an aggressive advertising and sampling campaign that catapulted the brand to major success.

Because they could produce their tequila cheaply, they could afford to be aggressive with their pricing. They only produced Reposado tequila, so they focused all their attention and advertising dollars on that single category. Within no time, Cazadores tequila had taken a large bite out of Sauza's Hornitos, the most popular Reposado tequila in Mexico. Cazadores' success has spawned a host of imitators, including El Jimador, 30-30, and El Charro. Recently, Cazadores has been forced to follow the trend of making 100% agave tequila, and in 1997, they began producing their own 100% agave tequila.

Tasting Notes

Cazadores Reposado: Pale yellow color. Full, mellow attack. *Sencillo*, with moderate agave intensity. Moderate caramel and smoke aromas, with slight hints of agave, pepper, fruit, and floral elements. Medium body and sweet in the mouth. The flavor is oaky with moderate agave and some pepper, but the major component tastes like dough or cardboard, possibly from the new oak barrels. The finish is moderately long and sweet, with that doughy taste lingering through the tingly alcohol.

Centinela
Cabrito
(NOM 1140)

Centinela is a family-owned business with claims of producing handcrafted tequilas dating back to 1894. Located in the city of Arandas, in the heart of the Los Altos tequila growing region, Centinela is supervised by master distiller Jaime Antonio Gonzales Torres. Don Jaime has supervised Centinela production for more than 30 years.

For several years, Centinela maintained an average production of around 3,000 liters per day, but it expanded dramatically to 15,000 liters per day by the end of 1996. Centinela owns some agave fields, but purchases the majority of its agaves from local farmers.

Hospitality at Centinela is warm and generous. Juan Leonardo Hernandez, the administrative manager, speaks no English, but lives to accommodate visitors, and has an unfailing palate for recommending fine restaurants in the area. A tour reveals a distillery bursting at the seams with a jumble of new *hornos,* tanks squeezed into cramped buildings, and stills fighting like saplings for a place in the sun. Every building on the property is filled from floor to ceiling with barrels.

All Centinela tequilas are 100% blue agave. Under the Centinela brand is a Blanco, a Reposado, an Añejo, and an Añejo Tres Años that is aged in barrel for three years. These tequilas are imported into the United States by El Dorado Importers. The second label, Cabrito, includes a Blanco and a Reposado, and has been distributed in the United States since 1996.

The house style is refined, gentle, and full of finesse, with pure, intense agave aromas and flavors, and rich, cream soda character in the aged tequilas. Delicately fresh, with layers of complexity hanging on a strong agave base, Centinela tequilas are favorites.

Tasting Notes

Centinela Blanco: Brilliant, colorless with a delicately complex *macho* attack. Intense earthy agave and wet cement aromas with honeysuckle and citrus. Flavors include light pepper laced with soft vanilla, and cinnamon spice on top of the agave. Slightly sweet, it is soft and viscous in the mouth. It finishes clean, with a long-lasting fruity flavor, and a burn that singes the tongue.

Centinela Reposado: Pale yellow color, with wow! intensity and some pungency on the attack. Definitely *macho* and *suave.* Wet cement and white pepper aromas dominate, backed up with good fruit and oak. Slightly sweet with a medium mouth feel. Agave is also at the front of flavor with moderate oak, caramel and pepper. The finish has little bitterness and sweetness. The flavors of caramel and agave last a long time, with a slight alcohol burn.

Centinela Añejo: Light golden color. *Macho* intensity and *suave* complexity with a mellow attack. White pepper and light smoke, combined with vanilla and caramel (cream soda) in the nose. Plenty of delicate, earthy agave aromas and flavors. Flavors are a nice balance of fruit, floral, and oak elements. Caramel, vanilla, and smoke mix together for a long-lasting, gentle finish.

Centinela Tres Años: Yellow gold color with a strong, but mellow attack. *Macho* intensity and great complexity. Delicate agave aromas, with more vanilla, toast, pepper, and caramel than the Añejo. The flavor includes spice, white pepper, smoke, cream soda, and butter, all balanced by earthy agave. Sweet in the mouth, with a creamy texture, it finishes with a lively pepper flavor.

Cabrito Blanco: Strong and mellow on the attack. Colorless. Moderate agave intensity and *sencillo*. Moderate agave aromas with some fruity character and hints of pepper and chamomile. Sweet and almost oily in the mouth. The moderate agave and pepper flavors quickly lose ground to a doughy, cardboard taste. The finish is moderately bitter. Flavors are short except for the dough flavor. Alcohol is hot.

Cabrito Reposado: This pale yellow tequila is full and mellow on the attack, with *macho* intensity and *suave* complexity. High agave aromas are backed with good fruit and pepper character, and slight hints of caramel and chamomile. The mouth feel is slightly sweet and slightly oily. Caramel and agave command attention in the flavor, and hints of cardboard linger in the background. The finish is slightly bitter, of medium length, and hot with toasty, doughy flavors.

El Charro
(NOM 1235)

Javier López can usually be found hanging out at La Penita Restaurant on the main square in Arandas. Drop in for a cup of the best coffee in town, and see if he's there. If not, cross the square diagonally and you'll find the brand new tasting room featuring his tequila, El Charro. El Charro tequila began production in 1996.

The distillery is six miles from town, down a bumpy and dusty road. Modern, new, and linked up to the computer age, El Charro tequila is produced by Arturo Fuentes. Arturo has 21 years of experience in the liquor business working for Martell Cognac, Ron Potosí, and Cuervo. Talented, experienced, and opinionated, Arturo represents the new, technical *tequilero.*

For example, El Charro uses a special machine to split the *piñas* and remove the flavorless central core. The *piñas* are cooked in 20-ton *hornos* lined with stainless steel. The *piñas* steam for 20 hours, and then the *aguamiel* is pumped to the fermenters. The remaining *piñas* are cooked another 12 hours before they are milled and mixed with water. Of course, this second cooking is heresy to the traditional *tequileros,* but Arturo is so confident and knowledgeable that everyone is paying attention.

I continue to see parallels between the tequila industry and the California wine industry. In the 1970s, winemakers trained at the University of California, Davis, moved into the wine business with a vengeance.

They brought all kinds of technical know-how, but very little experience. Traditional winemakers were dismayed at the inexperience of the newcomers and were slow to embrace new methodology. It took 10 to 15 years before this new technology was tempered by traditional methods leading to higher quality wine.

The tequila business is experiencing that same conflict between tradition and technology. Mexicano culture and machismo do not lend themselves to shared information, but somehow Javier López and his *tequilero* Arturo Fuentes remain well liked by all of the old tequila families of Arandas. Perhaps they will forge that link between technology and tradition.

Tasting Notes

El Charro Reposado: Pale yellow color, with full intensity and pungent on attack. Complex agave with moderate to *macho* intensity. Earthy agave aromas dominate, with definite notes of white pepper and citrus. There is a bit of sweetness, but the mouth feel is thin. The first flavor to hit is caramel, closely followed by agave, pepper, and oak. The aftertaste is medium sweet and hot from alcohol. Smoke and oak dominate a short finish.

Chinaco
(NOM 1127)

In the early 1970s, all tequila had to come from the state of Jalisco, but in 1973 Mexican government officials decided to expand tequila designation. They were intent on providing enough blue agave plants to meet future demands. They saw tequila as a unique product that brought in dollars and other foreign currencies.

One of the new areas, the northern state of Tamaulipas, was so designated in honor of the father of modern Mexican agrarian reform, Guillermo Gonzalez Diaz Lombardi. Representatives of one of the large distilleries in Tequila signed an agreement with the farmers of Tamaulipas promising to pay high prices for the agave. The farmers of Tamaulipas planted many hectares of blue agave, but after 8–10 years, when the agaves finally were ready for harvest, the major tequila producer backed out of the agreement.

The farmers had no buyer for their agaves. Guillermo Gonzalez refused to sell his agaves for less than promised. Rather than capitulate to what he felt was essentially blackmail, Gonzalez decided to build his own distillery and to make tequila using the agave plants of Tamaulipas. He picked a vacant cotton gin as a location. He bought some used distilling equipment and hired a *tequilero* reputed to have some experience, and a tiny distillery named *La Gonzaleña* was born.

La Gonzaleña's tequila was called Chinaco, named after the legendary defenders of Mexico during the Guerra de Reforma (War of Reform) in the 1850s. Chinaco tequila was born out of struggle, and has fought ever since to survive as the only tequila produced in Tamaulipas.

Chinaco tequila was introduced to the United States in 1983 by Robert Denton and Company. Denton marketed the tequila like a fine cognac, and demanded the highest prices of any tequila on the market. The rich, elegant Chinaco Añejo lived up to the promises, and almost single handedly created the North American market for upscale tequila.

The distillery closed in the late 1980s, and the remaining supply of Chinaco was quickly exhausted. Happily, under the guidance of Gonzalez's four sons, *La Gonzaleña* distillery was reborn, and Chinaco reappeared for sale in the United States in 1994. Currently Chinaco is available in three styles. The Blanco is bottled without any wood aging. The Reposado is aged in barrel for up to a year. The Añejo ages in oak barrels for up to four years.

The Chinaco house style is characterized by heavy, earthy agave aromas and flavors with solid fruit and floral hints. The tequilas are dry, not sweet, with a rich, full-bodied texture. The Añejo has a velvety, oily character. The oak aging regimen contributes nice caramel and vanilla accents, but doesn't overpower the bold agave. These bold, full-flavored tequilas are not designed for the timid.

Tasting Notes

Chinaco Blanco: The attack is full and mellow, with *muy macho* intensity and *suave* complexity. The aroma is complex with moderate amounts of white pepper, citrus, chamomile, and smoke layered with hints of caramel and loads of earthy agave. The mouth feel is medium and dry. The flavors follow the aroma. Spice, fruit, floral, and caramel add support to deep, earthy agave flavors. The hot finish is medium to long, with little bitterness and moderate sweetness. The finishing flavor is pure agave with hints of smoke and cream soda.

Chinaco Reposado: This also is full and mellow on the attack. A pretty, pale yellow color carries a *macho* intensity and *suave* complexity. The aromas have bits of everything dominated by agave and white pepper, built on layers of smoke and floral aromas, with touches of fruit and caramel. The mouth feel is medium and barely sweet. The flavors have moderate spice and caramel, hints of fruit, floral, and oak, and loads of earthy agave— ¡ay caramba! The aftertaste is moderate in both bitterness and sweetness. Alcohol is hot and stays hot. Duration of flavor is medium with smoky agave flavors.

Chinaco Añejo: The Añejo shares the same attack, intensity, and complexity as its predecessors, but has graduated to a yellow color. The aromas are intense, dominated by earthy agave with a strong presence of pepper, citrus, chamomile, caramel, smoke, and butterscotch. The tequila is oily, yet dry, an amazing accomplishment. Huge agave and caramel flavors are balanced by fruit, floral, oak, and butterscotch, with a bit of white pepper. The aftertaste is low on bitterness and moderate on sweetness. The alcohol level is hot. Duration of flavors is long with agave and caramel.

Corralejo
(NOM 1368)

Corralejo is one of the rare tequila producers outside the state of Jalisco. Located in Pénjamo, in the state of Guanajuato, the Hacienda Corralejo dates back to 1755 and was built by Mayor Pedro Sanchez de Tagle, who is reputed to be the first maker of tequila in Mexico.

Leonardo Rodriguez, a glass bottle manufacturer, purchased the property in 1989. He refurbished the plant and opened the new facility in June of 1996. Corralejo was designed to attract tourists, and includes tours and tasting as part of its day-to-day operations.

Corralejo produces 100% blue agave tequilas exclusively, using traditional production methods. Agaves are roasted in *hornos*, milled, fermented, and then distilled in new copper stills imported from Spain. Their style emphasizes smoky, earthy agave aromas and flavors with a light mouth feel and finish. The Reposado was introduced into California in November 1997. An Añejo will be available in January 1998. Distribution will spread to other selected states as production increases.

Tasting notes

Corralejo Reposado: Golden brown in color, it is strong and pungent on the attack. *Sencillo* complexity and moderate intensity. High earthy agave and *mezcal*-like smoky aromas dominate. Thin in the mouth with low sweetness. The flavors are earthy, smoky, and doughy. The finish is of medium length with tingly alcohol.

Jose Cuervo
Dos Reales
(NOM 1104)

Jose Cuervo Tequila is big. That's the first thing you have to understand. Jose Cuervo accounts for more than one-third of all tequila produced in Mexico. In other words, one out of every three bottles of tequila produced in the entire country of Mexico carries the Jose Cuervo name. Even more remarkable, 42% of all the tequila sold in the United States (more than 2 million cases in 1996), is Jose Cuervo, which puts it in the top ten list of all spirits sold, in the same league as giants like Bacardi, Smirnoff, and Jim Beam.

Jose Cuervo Tequila is also old, with 200 years of history as Mexico's oldest continuously running tequila distiller. Jose Maria Guadalupe Cuervo received a permit in 1795 allowing him to manufacture *mezcal* wine. That humble permit eventually led to the dynasty that is the present day Jose Cuervo. When Jose Guadalupe Cuervo died, the property went to his daughter, who gave control to her husband Vincente Albino Rojas. He modernized the distillery, expanded production and sales, and renamed the plant *La Rojeña*. Different heirs controlled the company through the 1800s. Jose Cuervo Labastida ran the operation from 1900–1921. Thereafter, a series of administrators ran the company, until the operation was returned to the Cuervo heirs.

The company is currently operated by Juan Beckmann Vidal, in partnership with Hueblein Corporation. Cuervo has two distilleries. A huge distillery and bottling plant sits just outside Guadalajara, but the one to visit is *La Rojeña*, located in the heart of Tequila. *La Rojeña* is a charming distillery, immaculately groomed, accented with brilliant magenta bougainvillea. A bank of *hornos* is in constant operation, steaming the agaves brought by an endless line of trucks. Rooms full of stainless steel tanks fermenting the *aguamiel* give off the heady spiced-yam aroma of cooked agave. A truly impressive distillation room glistens with polished copper alambic stills. The whole place features gardens and tile work of the first quality. Even the sign-in procedure, where they issue hard hats for the tour, adds to the charm.

It is virtually impossible to get any exact information about production details from Jose Cuervo. Most of their production is 51% agave *mixto* tequila. Cuervo Tradicional and Reserva de la Familia are the only 100% blue agave products. The second label, a *mixto* tequila called Dos Reales, is now a 100% agave brand called Gran Centenario.

The house style at Cuervo is sweet. The Blanco offers intense white pepper in the nose and the taste. Caramel aromas and flavors dominate the other tequilas.

Tasting Notes

Cuervo Silver: Colorless. The attack is wow! and pungent, with light one-dimensional agave intensity. The aroma is dominated by white pepper, with underlying notes of citrus, floral, and cardboard. Sweet, but thin in the mouth. High white pepper gives way to a hot alcoholic burn in the finish that lingers for quite some time.

Cuervo Especial (Gold): Faded gold with brown overtones. Light agave intensity. Intense caramel and vanilla aromas in the nose, with hints of agave and smoke. Very thick, heavy viscosity, with buttery, toasty flavors. Cloyingly sweet on the finish.

Cuervo 1800: Golden with brown tones. Full attack, but light agave intensity. *Sencillo.* Lots of caramel and vanilla aromas, to the point of cream soda in the nose. Sweet with medium mouth feel. Nutty, caramel flavors. More delicate than Cuervo Especial

Cuervo Tradicional: Clear with some brown tones. Strong attack with a burn. *Macho* agave intensity. Earthy, wet cement aromas, with smoke and slight caramel. Sweet and full in the mouth. Mild agave flavor, some smoke, and definite volatile flavors lead to a long bitter finish that remains hot.

Cuervo Reserva de la Familia: Dark gold and brown. Full, mellow attack. Light agave intensity and *sencillo* agave complexity. Loads of toasty oak with plenty of smoke in the aroma. Sweet and oily in the mouth. Toasty, oaky, and smoky flavors with some caramel, but minimal agave flavor. After the initial flavors hit, a jolt of hot alcohol takes over, but soon dissipates. Tastes very much like slightly sweet bourbon, with a long caramel and cardboard finish.

Dos Reales Blanco: Colorless with a light, mellow attack. Light agave intensity with *sencillo* complexity. Perfumed floral and citrus notes in the aroma give way to slight acetone aromas and some pepper. Very sweet and hot in the mouth. Slight pepper and smoke flavors leading to a sweet, hot finish.

Dos Reales Añejo: Golden with hints of brown. Light and mellow attack, with light agave intensity and *sencillo* agave complexity. Caramel aromas dominate with wisps of smoke and a solid hit of acetone aromas. Sweet in the mouth, with slight anise and toast flavors that quickly give way to lip-numbing alcohol. Sweet cardboard flavors and heat dominate the finish.

Herradura
El Jimador
(NOM 1119)

Tequila Herradura was founded in 1861 by Feliciano Romo in Amatitan, a small hillside town about six miles south of the town of Tequila. According to the family history, while Feliciano was looking for a building site for his distillery, he caught a glint of light flashing in the ground. Closer inspection revealed an old horseshoe, and thus the site was selected. The brand name, Herradura, means horseshoe in Spanish.

The original distillery has been transformed into a museum through the efforts of the Romo family. Both the original distillery and the current ultra-modern one are situated on the family estate, San José del Refugio, in Amatitan. Guillermo "Bill" Romo is the current general manager.

Modeled after a small European estate, Herradura grows all of its own agave on 10 thousand acres containing some eight million agave plants. Current production is four million liters annually, and about 75% is sold in Mexico. Herradura projects 10–12% annual growth for the next ten years to reach an annual production of nine million liters.

All Herradura tequilas are made from 100% blue agave. Herradura ferments, distills, ages, and bottles its tequilas on the premises without additives, sugars, or colorings. Herradura has earned the right to use the legal terms "natural" and "estate bottled" on its U.S. labels.

Herradura successfully combines traditional and state-of-the-art tequila making methods. They have pioneered research into yeast types to carry on the initial fermentation of the *aguamiel*. Their attention to cleanliness and sterility in the production process has set the standard for the industry. They continue to experiment and test for new techniques in their quest to make some of Mexico's finest tequilas.

Herradura produces four classes of tequila: Silver, Reposado (Gold), Añejo, and Seleccion Suprema. The Silver receives little or no wood aging, while the Reposado averages three to eleven months in oak barrels. The Añejo tequila is aged for one to four years in barrel, and the new Seleccion Suprema (first released in 1996) is aged for five years. Their new El Jimador brand (currently available only in Mexico but due for release in the United States by 1997), is Reposado tequila aged two to three months in oak barrels. Plans include expanding the El Jimador line to include a Blanco and a Gold tequila.

The Herradura house style is intense, concentrated agave with lots of oak flavor in their aged tequilas. The tequilas are made from very ripe agaves, and exhibit complex aromas and flavors, with some nuances of distillate compounds like ethyl acetate or aldehyde. The barrel aging regimen at Herradura sacrifices fresh agave character for more complex wood-related flavors like caramel and smoke. The oldest tequilas (Añejo and Suprema) more closely resemble fine cognacs.

Tasting Notes

Herradura Blanco: This colorless tequila has a wow! and pungent attack. Light to moderate agave intensity is overwhelmed by other complex aromas, such as the moderate earthy aroma, slight amounts of spice, citrus, and floral scents, and loads of distilled aromas like ethyl acetate. It has a nice, full feel on the tongue with slight sweetness, followed by an astringent drying of the palate. Moderate earth and pepper with slight floral flavors are dominated by the heavy distilled flavors. Aftertaste is surprisingly short, with no single flavor at the forefront.

Herradura Reposado: Light yellow color, and strong on the attack. Pungent with sharp ripe apple aromas and hints of acetone. Also highly caramelized, with moderate smoke, floral and agave aromas. Sweet on the entry with rich, earthy agave flavor and some dry doughy flavors. The finish is long with smoky agave and a bourbon-like aftertaste.

Herradura Añejo: Golden in color, this tequila is strong on attack and slightly pungent. Moderate agave intensity is overwhelmed by wood aging character. Moderate earthy aromas, slightly spicy, fruity, and floral, with loads of oaky, caramelized aromas, and a prominent heavy, ripe apple aroma. Medium body in the mouth, full but not sweet. Slight to moderate earthy agave flavors, with slight pepper and *¡ay caramba!* levels of oak and caramel flavor. Long oaky finish, reminiscent of a good bourbon whisky.

Herradura Seleccion Suprema: A definite wow! on the attack with pungent aromas. Dark gold color. *¡Ay caramba!* levels of oaky, smoky, cream soda aromas mask agave intensity. Hints of white pepper and citrus show through. Almost oily in the mouth, the tequila is slightly sweet. Flavors follow the aromas: slight earthy agave and pepper, loads of caramel and oak. The finish is long with no bitterness, full of sweet oak and whisky flavors.

El Jimador Reposado: Strong attack and slightly pungent, this tequila is a pretty yellow color. *Macho* intensity and *suave* complexity lead to high levels of earthy agave with moderate pepper, fruit, chamomile, and caramel aromas. The mouth feel is medium with a low level of sweetness. Flavors are balanced between agave, caramel, and pepper with hints of fruit and smoke. The aftertaste is moderately sweet and moderately bitter. Duration of flavor is medium with a long, hot finish.

Jalisciense
El Amo Aceves
30-30
(NOM 1068)

Typical of the entire modern Mexicano tequila business, Agroindustrias Guadalajara is a cooperative of 17 growers who formed their own company in 1994. Theirs was the first new tequila license taken out in more than a decade, and they pre-date the recent flood of newly formed tequila companies. They constructed a new distillery in the town of Capilla de Guadalupe, halfway between Arandas and Tepatitlan, in the Los Altos region.

The facility is modern and spotless with plenty of room for growth. As of 1997 it contains two 16–18 ton autoclaves, three 3,500-liter stills, with production capabilities of five thousand liters per day. All tequila is 100% blue agave, and the bulk of the agaves are farmed by the partners.

Sounds pretty straightforward, right?

Heriberto Gomez is the president and director of the company. Working as production manager is Elpidio Aceves. Together they released their first offering of tequila in 1995. Called 30-30 (Treinta-Treinta), the tequila is currently available as a Reposado only, aged in oak for two months.

Javier Aceves, Elpidio's brother, was hired to market 30-30. He says he got it started, but then decided to strike out on his own with the Jalisciense label. Once the Jalisciense brand got rolling, Javier started his upscale premium band, El Amo Aceves, an Añejo elaborately packaged in a rectangular, clear glass bottle with a small genuine silver agave plant attached.

Additionally, by the summer of 1997, Agroindustrias Guadalajara was making the Las Trancas brand, previously produced at El Viejito, in Atotonilco. Another brand called Ambarfino is under development, specially designed for a major United States liquor distributor, although they won't say which one.

All these tequilas are produced at the same plant with Elpidio Aceves as the production manager. The agaves come from the various 17 partners. I've been told that different production techniques apply to the various brands, but the owners refuse to divulge their secrets. The house style features good agave character, especially in the aromas, decent caramel notes from the aging, but a pretty high burn from the alcohol.

Tasting Notes

Jalisciense Reposado: Strong and pungent attack. Yellow color, with *macho* intensity and *suave* complexity. Lots of caramel and agave in the nose. Slightly sweet in the mouth with medium mouth feel. Pepper and alcohol are the dominant flavors with some pepper. The finish is long, but bitter with the alcohol building to lip-numbing intensity.

Jalisciense Añejo: Strong, pungent attack, with a golden color and moderate agave intensity. High smoke followed by high agave aromas, with bits of caramel and floral notes. Slightly sweet with thin to medium mouth feel. The flavor is dominated by pepper and alcohol. This baby is definitely lip-numbing and finishes with some bitterness.

El Amo Aceves Añejo: Light golden color with a strong and mellow attack. *Macho* intensity and *suave* complexity. Caramel and earthy agave dominate the aroma, with moderate chamomile, and hints of smoke and pepper in the background. Low sweetness with medium mouth feel. The floral character comes to the fore in the taste, supported by good caramel and decent agave flavors. The flavors are short in the finish, taken over by hot to lip-numbing alcohol.

30-30 Reposado: Strong, mellow attack. Yellow with brown edges. *Suave* agave complexity with *macho* agave intensity. Excellent earthy agave aromas with hints of pepper, citrus, smoke, and caramel. Sweet with a medium mouth feel. Flavors are pepper, agave, and caramel. The finish is long and hot, dominated by flavors of wet cement and sweet caramel.

Orendain
(NOM 1110)

Orendain is the third grand old tequila family of Mexico. Located in the town of Tequila, their company dates back to the 1870s when it competed with Cuervo and Sauza as one of Mexico's largest premium tequila producers. In the early 1900s, the family left the business. Eduardo Orendain returned in 1935. The company is currently owned and operated by Eduardo's sons.

Orendain is alternately the third or the fourth largest exporter of tequila to the United States, with exports between four million and five million liters annually. You may be familiar with the labels Pepe Lopez or Puerto Vallarta. The bulk of the production is *mixto* tequila, with a small production of 100% agave tequila under the brand name of Ollitas.

Tasting Notes

Ollitas Reposado: Golden color. Strong and pungent on attack, *suave* complexity with *macho* intensity. Earthy, wet cement agave balances nicely with smoke aromas. Thin in the mouth with low sweetness. Flavor is primarily smoke and acetone with bits of earthy agave. Finish is medium with acetone and overripe apple flavors.

Porfidio
(several different producers)

Porfidio has one of the most unique stories in the tequila business. Its owner, Martin Grassl, successfully predicted the expanding export market for 100% blue agave tequilas. Using a series of different distilleries to produce his various tequilas along with some of the most dynamic packaging in the industry, Grassl took his Porfidio brand to great success in the United States.

Marketing and packaging are Porfidio's strong points. Porfidio is most famous for its hand-blown "cactus bottle," which actually contains a small glass cactus in every bottle. It seems not to matter that cactus has nothing to do with the production of tequila, and that this packaging encourages misinformation about the product. Grassl uses a different shaped bottle for each type of tequila he produces. His Añejo Extra comes in a ceramic bottle in the shape of a gourd with a replica of an agave plant adorning its surface. His Silver and Añejo tequilas come in different colored long-necked bottles labeled with modern designs in bold colors. Grassl even has a triple-distilled tequila, in a long-necked frosted bottle.

It may be difficult for consumers to know which distillery is producing their favorite bottle of Porfidio at any given time. Porfidio tequilas have been produced by the same distilleries who make El Viejito, Arette, Tres Alegres Compadres, Regional, and J. R. Reyes tequilas. You can track your favorite Porfidio tequilas back to their original distillery if the bottle has an NOM number.

The future of Porfidio will at least be interesting. I have never met Mr. Grassl, but I have talked to the owner of one distillery who has produced Porfidio in the past. He told me he is considering legal action against Mr. Grassl. I have also contacted Porfidio's former distributor in the United States. They refuse to discuss the matter on advice of their attorneys. Rumors of additional lawsuits continue to circulate. Whether some of this legal entanglement is due to jealously on the part of rivals, I don't know, but tequila is already a volatile beverage. Introducing lawyers into the mix could be incendiary.

Tasting Notes

Porfidio Silver: Full and mellow on the attack, this colorless tequila has moderate agave intensity. Moderate agave aromas along with a dried grass floral character. Slightly sweet with medium mouth feel, the flavors are earthy agave, pepper, and anise. The finish is tingly, of medium length, and slightly sweet.

Porfidio Añejo (2 year): Golden color with a strong, pungent attack. *Macho* agave intensity. Moderate wet cement agave with some caramelized aromas that are overpowered by the hot burn of alcohol. A hint of sweetness and a full mouth feel. Smoke, caramel, and earthy agave flavors. A long, hot finish that mellows into a caramel and smoke aftertaste.

Porfidio Single Barrel Añejo: Gold color with a strong, pungent attack. *Macho* and *suave*. Intense ginseng agave layered with caramel, pepper, and toasty oak aromas. Slightly sweet and full in the mouth. Flavors start with sweet caramel and agave, but burst into a long, smooth, smoky, caramel finish.

Porfidio Añejo Extra: Yellow in color, with a strong, pungent attack. A sharp mineral, vegetal aroma redolent of overripe apple overwhelms the modest agave in the nose. Light and thin in the mouth. Vegetal and mineral flavors. A short, flat finish with very little heat. There is a slight aftertaste of cooked vegetables.

Pueblo Viejo
San Matias
(NOM 1103)

One of the great historical distilleries, San Matias was founded in the 1880s near the town of Tequila. Owner Delfino González started the original distillery on his Rancho San Matias. Over the years, he developed the business, built additional distilleries, and created the San Matias brand, especially successful in northern Mexico.

In 1958, Delfino brought in Guillermo Castañeda as a partner. Together, they moved the company to Tepatitlan in the Los Altos area, where Castañeda directed the company to national success until he retired in 1985. He sold the company to Jesus Lopez.

Lopez launched a new brand, Pueblo Viejo. Made from 100% blue agave, Pueblo Viejo found instant acceptance, especially in the state of Jalisco. Every taxi driver I talked with recommended Pueblo Viejo Tequila. San Matias also does well as a *mixto* tequila, but is hard to find in the United States—more than 98% of its sales are in Mexico.

Lopez was an outspoken critic who demanded enforcement of regulations concerning the amount of agave used in tequila production. In June of 1997, Jesus Lopez was brutally assassinated in front of his distillery. At this writing, his murder remains unsolved. The future of both Pueblo Viejo and San Matias does not look bright.

Tasting Notes

San Matias Reposado: Light golden color with a full, pungent attack. Light agave intensity. The aromas are completely dominated by pungent, smoky, cooked vegetable smells. Medium sweet with medium mouth feel. Flavors are vegetal with caramel and smoke. Very hot finish gives way to a burnt cardboard aftertaste.

Pueblo Viejo Blanco: Colorless, full, and slightly pungent on the attack. Light agave intensity and *sencillo* agave complexity. Herbal, artichoke, and ripe apple aromas dominate. Low sweetness and thin to medium mouth feel. Some pepper and sweet caramel flavors with hints of agave. Hot, medium finish with a sweet, apple flavor.

Pueblo Viejo Reposado: Pale yellow color with a moderate, pungent attack. *Sencillo* complexity with moderate agave intensity. Some earthy agave aromas are mixed with smoke, caramel, and bits of pepper. Sweet and full in the mouth. Caramel and earthy agave flavors dominate. The finish is hot with long-lasting flavors of white pepper that turn to caramel.

Regional
(NOM 1121)

The cooperative distillery Regional has recently begun to promote its own brand. In the past, the distillery has produced tequilas for various people, the most famous being Porfidio's Añejo tequila in the cactus bottle.

Located directly across the street from the famous Herradura property, Regional has long played the forgotten stepchild of tequila in Amatitan. The plant remains small, producing less than 100 thousand liters of tequila annually. However, they currently have the capacity to triple that production.

This particular cooperative has been slow to develop. With many different growers trying to make decisions and further various agendas, management has turned over frequently. Hopefully, they have now come together for the common good, and will eventually garner some of the attention their tequilas deserve.

Tasting Notes

Regional Reposado: Strong and mellow on the attack with *macho* intensity and *suave* complexity, this golden tequila is loaded with earthy agave and caramelized aromas, with moderate citrus notes, hints of white pepper, and chamomile. Almost oily in the mouth, but with low sweetness, agave is the key flavor, with moderate smoke and white pepper flavors in the background. The finish is hot and long, with a distinctive smoke and caramel aftertaste.

Tequila Sauza
(NOM 1102)

After Jose Cuervo, Tequila Sauza is Mexico's second largest producer of tequila. In 1873 Don Cenobio Sauza purchased several distilleries, intent on becoming a major tequila producer. His son Eladio Sauza ran the company after Don Cenobio's death. Eladio expanded and upgraded *La Perseverancia*, his father's first distillery purchase, until it has now become the Sauza showplace. Eladio's son Javier broadened distribution and built Sauza into Mexico's second largest exporter of bulk tequila. Javier ran the company until Domecq acquired the company in 1987.

La Perseverancia is a large, modern distillery in the town of Tequila. Agave *piñas* pass directly from the trucks to a shredder. The shredded agave pulp moves by conveyor to upright autoclaves, where the pulp cooks in a quick eight hours. The *aguamiel* is pumped to large stainless steel vats for fermentation. The tequila is distilled in 4,000-liter stills.

Just a few miles down the road from the distillery is *Rancho El Indio*, Sauza's experimental agave plantation. It offers visitors the best explanation of the agave growing process, complete with demonstrations of the planting, selection, and harvest of the hijuelos, and the subsequent harvest of mature agave. Examples of various planting regimens, displays of the tools, and a tasting bar make *Rancho El Indio* a prime destination for any true tequila aficionado.

The Sauza house style is primarily *mixto*, with modest agave character and a solid sweetness (but not as sweet as Cuervo). The high-end tequilas have more complexity, with medicinal notes, a firm agave structure, and solid oak flavors.

Tasting Notes

Sauza Silver: Colorless. Strong and pungent on the attack. Moderate agave intensity, *sencillo* complexity. White pepper dominates the aroma, with modest agave and hints of floral character and acetone. Sweet and light in the mouth. Flavor is mostly white pepper. The finish is short and harsh.

Sauza Especial: Golden with a brown tinge, this tequila is full and pungent. Moderate intensity and *sencillo* complexity. Aromas of burnt caramel and dried grass dominate some doughy cardboard smells. Sweet and thick in the mouth with heavy toasty flavors up front that fall apart into a sweet, hot finish.

Sauza Conmemorativo: Pale yellow color, with a strong and pungent attack. Moderate agave intensity, *suave* complexity. Aromas of moderate ginseng agave, white pepper and strong hints of iodine. White pepper, vanilla, agave, and some iodine in the flavors. Sweet and medium mouth feel, leading to a long, complex finish of vanilla, white pepper, and iodine, reminiscent of blended scotch.

Sauza Hornitos: Pale golden color. Strong, mellow attack, with moderate, *sencillo* agave complexity. Caramel, earthy agave, and pepper aromas, followed by citrus and lilac. Sweet and full in the mouth.

Caramel, agave, and pepper flavors. Aftertaste is long and tingly with just a hint of smoky bitterness. One of the best dollar for dollar values for 100% blue agave tequila.

Sauza Tres Generaciones: Pale gold color with moderate agave intensity and a mellow, full attack. Caramel aromas with some pepper and floral character. Sweet and oily in the mouth. Lots of smoke flavor with some pepper and a lot of acetone and overripe apple elements. Very hot finish with a long, smoky flavor.

Sauza Tres Generaciones 100% Agave: This new version of Tres Generaciones first appeared in 1997. Pungent and full on attack, this pale gold tequila shows moderate agave intensity and *suave* complexity. Moderate earthy agave and caramel are dominated by dry floral aromas. Sweet in the mouth with medium mouth feel, the dominant flavors are pepper and oak with slight agave, fruit, and floral notes. The finish is short and hot leading to moderate bitterness.

Galardon Gran Reposado: Sauza's newest entry into the 100% blue agave market, Galardon is light and mellow on the attack, and shows moderate intensity and *sencillo* complexity. Caramel and agave aromas are prominent, with hints of floral and spice. Slightly sweet and thin in the mouth. Agave and caramel flavors give way to a dry herbal flavor. Moderately sweet and hot on the finish with a long-lasting herbal flavor.

Siete Leguas
Patrón
(NOM 1120)

Siete Leguas (Seven Leagues) dates back to the 1920s. Currently, Lucretia González and her son Fernando operate the business. Siete Leguas has two distilleries in the town of Atotonilco—a smaller plant with traditional *hornos* and *tahona,* and a more modern facility that produces the bulk of Siete Leguas tequila.

Siete Leguas rose to fame as the first producer of Patrón tequila. Released as a Blanco and an Añejo, the Patrón brand is owned by Martin Crowley of St. Maarten Spirits Company. Crowley worked with the Siete Leguas production manager to develop the first blend of Patrón Añejo. The first Patrón Blanco defined the classic wet cement, earthy character of tequila made from Los Altos agave. Patrón's beautiful, distinctive hand-blown glass bottle proved a great success in the United States. It set the trend for a wave of high-priced tequila in designer bottles.

Crowley attempted a joint venture with Siete Leguas, but that didn't work out. Eventually, he signed a distribution deal with Seagrams Company. Sales quickly exceeded production. Siete Leguas could not meet the demand, especially for the Añejo. Because Patrón continues as one of the most successful ultra-premium brands in the United States, Crowley is considering using other distilleries to produce additional supplies.

On its own, Siete Leguas is a renowned tequila

producer in Mexico. The house style features full-blown, in-your-face wet cement agave aromas and flavors. The Blanco tequila is the freshest and purest example. Reposados and Añejos pick up some fine complex flavors, but remain a bit harsh and rustic.

Tasting Notes

Patrón Blanco: Wow! and pungent, this colorless tequila explodes with classic wet cement agave aromas. *Muy macho* intensity and very *suave*, with hints of lemon, pepper, and banana in the background. Oily with some sweetness, it tastes like it smells: wet cement, earthy, complex agave. The finish is hot and long with a hint of sweetness accompanying the agave.

Patrón Añejo: Strong and pungent/burning on attack, this tequila is golden in color. Complex and *muy macho*. Earthy agave aromas dominate, with lots of toasty caramel from the oak. Definite hints of citrus and some pepper. Oily in the mouth, with little sweetness. Flavors fall off to cardboard, ripe apples, caramel, and creosote. The finish is long and hot with some bitterness. Cardboard, doughy flavors last a long time.

Siete Leguas Reposado: Pale yellow color, pungent and full. *Macho* agave intensity with good complexity. Agave, ginseng, and caramel are the primary aromas along with burning alcohol. Slightly sweet and full in the mouth. Caramel and toasty oak flavors overlay the earthy agave and ginseng. The finish is hot, with the caramel flavors of medium duration.

Siete Leguas Añejo: Golden color with a full, pungent attack. Moderate, *suave* agave intensity. Toasty oak is the strongest aroma, laced with earthy agave, caramel, and pepper. Low sweetness and medium mouth feel. Smoke and caramel jump out in the flavor, followed by agave. The finish is lip-numbing with a long-lasting smoke and caramel aftertaste.

Tapatio
El Tesoro
(NOM #1139)

The El Tesoro brand, known in Mexico as Tequila Tapatio, is owned by the Camarena family. The Camarenas have produced tequila near the town of Arandas, since 1937, with patriarch Don Felipe taking control in 1971. Don Felipe is still active, but the daily operation is being turned over to his son, Carlos.

Their distillery, *La Alteña*, is a working museum surrounded by dramatic construction ongoing since 1995. All agaves used for El Tesoro tequila come from the Camarenas' agave fields. They own more than two thousand acres of land planted to 2.5 million agaves. Agaves are selectively harvested according to ripeness. They are split and then slow cooked in traditional *hornos* for 48 hours. After a 24-hour cooling period, the *piñas* are pulverized by a tractor-drawn stone *tahona*. The pulp is hand carried in wooden buckets to wooden tanks, where it is diluted for fermentation. After a three-to five-day fermentation, the *aguamiel* is again hand carried to the stills. The first distillation includes the pulp. The second distillation is completed in a tiny 500-liter still. El Tesoro tequilas are distilled to proof, approximately 42% alcohol. Visiting *La Alteña* is a must for any true tequila aficionado.

El Tesoro is imported into the United States by Robert Denton and Company. Denton and his partner, Marilyn Smith, have almost single-handedly educated North America about fine tequilas, and the El Tesoro and Chinaco brands have become industry standards. They have fought for consistency in labeling and for adherence to Mexican law governing the proper use of agave in tequila production.

El Tesoro tequilas are rugged with powerful, earthy agave flavors and aromas. Aged tequilas are blended from several different batches of tequila, so oak remains an accent rather than an overpowering component. Rich, viscous, and complex, El Tesoro is not subtle, but it is intensely representative of Los Altos agave and tequila.

Tasting Notes

El Tesoro Plata: Brilliantly clear. Wow! intensity and pungent on the attack. *Muy macho* and *suave* intensity. Intense earthy agave character, like pavement after a summer rain. Smoky with floral notes in the aroma. Sweet, thick, and viscous in the mouth. White pepper and lemon flavors mix with the agave. Harsh and hot in the finish.

El Tesoro Añejo: Lovely yellow gold color. Wow! and pungent. *Macho* and *suave* agave intensity. Intense agave aromas redolent with earth, smoke, and caramel. Butter, caramel, toast, and vanilla flavors swirl around the strong agave flavor base. Slightly sweet with a medium mouth feel. The finish is hot, with long-lasting agave flavor and hints of pepper and lemon.

El Tesoro-Paradiso: This Añejo tequila, aged five years in oak, has a beautiful golden color. Wow! on the attack and mellow and soft. *Suave* complexity with *macho* intensity. The aromas show high levels of earthy, wet cement agave and oak, enhanced with moderate levels of fruit, spice, and caramel. There is a sumptuous oily feel in the mouth in spite of low sweetness. The flavors are agave and oak, with moderate fruit, pepper, and overripe apple. Medium bitterness and low sweetness in the finish leads to a long-lasting agave, oak finish that is marred by a persistent alcohol burn.

Tapatio Reposado: Yellow color with a strong, slightly pungent attack. *Muy macho* and *suave* agave intensity. Powerful wet cement agave aromas with lots of floral and citrus notes blended with hints of pepper and smoke. Low sweetness with a medium mouth feel. All elements of flavor are beautifully balanced, except the wet cement agave, which is the main attraction. The finish is tingly, featuring long-lasting agave flavor.

Tres Magueyes
Don Julio
(NOM 1118)

Tres Magueyes, located in the beautiful town of Atotonilco, produces fine Blanco and Reposado *mixto* tequilas that have long been respected in Mexico. The 100% blue agave brand, Don Julio, is a favorite, especially among North American tourists in Cancun. In fall of 1997, Tres Magueyes is scheduled to release Don Julio Real, which comes in a dramatic decanter bottle overlaid with a silver agave. The decanter sits in a polished steel replica of an alambic still and sells for 2,000 pesos, almost $270 US. A distribution deal with Rémy Martin is planned that should allow both labels to be distributed in the United States.

Marcos Cedano is the pleasant plant manager. He relies on Enrique Abarca to run the stills. Enrique has 35 years of experience at Tres Magueyes, and two of his brothers work at the plant with him. In fact, the nice thing about Tres Magueyes is that the whole place has a family feel about it. The plant operates at full capacity, but in such an organized and efficient manner that visitors have a sense of calm. The entire plant, while a long way from new, sparkles with cleanliness and neat organization.

The compact distillery is a mix of traditional and modern. Eight *hornos* cook agave for 36 hours. The *piñas* are milled, the juice is diluted, and fermentation finishes in 24 hours. For 100% blue agave tequila production, the first distillation takes approximately one hour, leaving the *ordinario* tequila at 26% alcohol. The second, three-hour distillation yields 60% alcohol. The *mixto* tequila begins with sweeter *aguamiel*, so the first distillation yields 35% alcohol. All distillations occur in stainless steel stills.

The Tres Magueyes style exhibits smooth, rich tequilas based on the undeniable agave aromas and flavors, interwoven with additional notes that add complexity. Well made, the tequilas are never aggressive.

Tasting Notes

Tres Magueyes Blanco: Strong and mellow on the attack, this colorless tequila has *macho* intensity and *suave* complexity. Lovely earthy, ginseng aromas with smoke and pepper. Little sweetness with medium body. Delicate flavors with hints of agave, earth, and smoke. The finish is hot, with long-lasting reminders of chamomile and earthy agave.

Tres Magueyes Reposado: Yellow with a full, mellow attack. *Macho* intensity and *suave* complexity. Cream soda aromas mix with earthy agave and overripe apple. Slightly sweet and full in the mouth. Vanilla, caramel, agave, and apple flavors. Tingly finish, with a hint of bitterness and a long duration of flavors.

Don Julio Reposado: Pale yellow in color with a strong, mellow attack. *Macho* and *muy suave* complexity. Delicate wet cement agave, caramel, and floral aromas, with hints of pepper and lemon. Low sweetness and medium body. Agave, apple, and caramel flavors, plus traces of pepper and dried flowers. The finish is hot and long-lasting. The aftertaste changes from a complex combination of agave, smoke, and caramel to almost pure cream soda.

El Viejito

Aguila

Hussong's

(NOM 1107)

El Viejito is a classic Mexicano tequila company. Claiming roots back to 1937, El Viejito is owned and operated by Antonio Nuñez. Antonio went to Texas Christian University on a Rotary scholarship, while his brother Jorge ran the company. In Texas, Antonio met, courted, and married his wife Ferril, and then returned to Mexico to take over the reins of the company in 1973. He currently runs the company with his son, Juan.

More than 90% of El Viejito's production is exported to foreign markets, such as the United States, Germany, Canada, Australia, Japan, and Chile. In 1996, El Viejito exported close to two million liters of tequila. Antonio Nuñez's company has been responsible for much of the recent worldwide popularity of tequila.

The company produces and exports the El Viejito label and several others, including Aguila, Las Trancas, Porfidio, Hussong's, Distinct, Sierra (the number one brand in Germany), Don Quixote, and Los Cinco Soles. As is typical in the current tequila market, Porfidio and Las Trancas have moved to other distilleries. El Viejito products have had several different distributors in the United States, but they have been unable to grab a foothold. Hussong's, once shipped in bulk to the United States and bottled by McCormick

Distillery labeled as 99% agave tequila, is now bottled and labeled at El Viejito as 100% agave tequila.

In 1987, Antonio Nuñez and David Kay started up a joint venture brand called Aguila. David Kay spent 20 years in the liquor business, specializing in various tequila brands, including the creation of Pepe Lopez tequila. He operated wholesale and retail operations in between stints as brand manager for companies like Sauza. The Aguila brand includes Blanco, Reposado, and Añejo *mixto* tequilas, along with a super-premium 100% blue agave Añejo packaged in a hand-blown blue glass bottle.

All of El Viejito's 100% blue agave tequilas show moderate to *macho* agave intensity and flavor, with pepper and citrus as secondary notes. The *mixto* tequilas, as should be expected, have less pronounced agave character, but remain solid examples of good, simple tequila.

Tasting Notes

El Viejito Blanco: Strong and mellow on the attack. Colorless with moderate agave intensity. A balance of earthy agave, white pepper, and citrus in the aroma. Sweet and medium-bodied in the mouth. Moderate agave and white pepper flavors with fruity, floral notes. The finish is hot and medium, but the duration of discernable flavor is short.

El Viejito Añejo: Golden color. Full, pungent attack with moderate, simple agave intensity. Agave, smoke, and caramel dominate the aromas with hints of pepper and floral character. Sweet with medium mouth feel.

Subdued flavors of caramel, smoke, and agave lead to a very hot, astringent finish. Long-lasting flavors of smoke and bitter pepper remain in the mouth.

Aguila Blanco: Colorless with a full, mellow attack. Moderate intensity with *suave* complexity. Intense agave dominates the aroma, with balanced measures of citrus, floral, pepper, and smoke. Sweet and medium mouth feel. Flavors are spice and pepper with slight agave and fruit. A short, hot finish with moderate bitterness.

Aguila Reposado: Full and mellow on the attack. Yellow color with simple agave and moderate intensity. Caramel and acetone notes cover slight agave, fruit, and caramel aromas. Sweet and medium in the mouth. Lots of caramel and oak flavors with decent agave. The finish is very hot and very sweet.

Aguila 100% Blue Agave: Strong and pungent, this Añejo tequila is golden with hints of brown. *Macho* intensity. Lots of agave along with well-balanced fruit, floral, and pepper in the aroma. Sweet and oily in the mouth. The flavors are first caramel, and then oak and agave. The finish is medium, hot, and sweet.

Hussong's Reposado: Pale yellow color. Strong and mellow on the attack with complex, *macho* intensity. Sweet and medium-full in the mouth. Lots of earthy, ginseng agave aromas with some smoke and pepper. Agave flavors with caramel, oak, and smoke. Alcohol is tingly, and the finish is medium with sweet agave and smoke flavors.

Viuda de Romero
Alteño
Real Hacienda
(NOM 1111)

Trying to follow the history of Viuda de Romero is enough to drive you to drink. The earliest recorded references to the Romero family's interest in tequila go all the way back to 1852 when Don Epitacio Romero produced "mescal wine." Don Epitacio died in 1873, leaving his estate to Don Francisco Romero Gonzalez. In 1888, Don Francisco formed a partnership with Don Cenobio Sauza and others. Over the next 45 years, no less than four different tequila distilleries were operated by various members of the Romero family. When Don Francisco died, his widow, Doña Catalina Aguilar Madrileño, became the *Viuda de Romero*—the Widow Romero of the brand name.

In 1933 Don Tomás Romero sold the rights to the Viuda de Romero name to the Velazco family, who later sold the brand to another producer named Gonzalez and Noriega. By 1976, the Viuda de Romero Company produced 14 registered brands and ran two distillation plants, one in Guadalajara and one in Tequila.

In 1979 Don Joaquin Gonzalez formed a partnership with a Spanish company called Cavas Back, who managed the brand until 1983, when they closed their Mexican operations and sold the business to L. A. Cetto, one of Mexico's most established wine producers. Louis Cetto completed construction of a new facility for Viuda de Romero in 1985. The current facility, located on the main highway just outside the town of Tequila, includes a distillery, barrel aging warehouse, bottling facility, corporate offices, and a tasting room.

At Viuda de Romero, agave is steamed in 15-ton autoclaves, and distilled in 3,000-liter stills that produce about five thousand liters per day. The Reposado tequila is aged six months in large oak tanks. The Añejo is aged for two years in oak barrels.

The Viuda de Romero brand includes a Blanco, Reposado, and Añejo—all 51% blue agave from both Tequila and Los Altos. At the same facility, they also produce Real Hacienda Silver, Reposado, and Añejo, all of which are 100% blue agave from Tequila and Los Altos. Finally, they have El Alteño, a 100% blue agave Reposado made exclusively from Los Altos agaves. In addition, the facility produces 8–10 other brands of tequila sold in Mexico and other countries.

Tasting Notes

Viuda de Romero Reposado: Full on the attack and slightly pungent, this yellow tequila presents *macho* intensity and good complexity. Powerful earthy agave aromas are followed by white pepper and hints of citrus, chamomile, and cream soda. Medium mouth feel and slightly sweet on the tongue. Loads of pepper flavor and almost as much earthy agave flavor. Moderate fruit and floral notes with a hint of caramel. The finish is hot, with a distinct bitter agave flavor of medium duration.

Viuda de Romero Añejo Inmemorial: Strong and pungent on the attack. Golden in color with moderate agave intensity. Oak and agave aromas dominate with lots of smoke layered on top of slight fruity, floral, and spicy aromas. Slightly thin in the mouth with no sweetness. Lots of oak flavor followed closely by white pepper and smoke, decent agave, caramel, and fruit flavors in the background. Low sweetness and bitterness on the finish, which is medium. The flavor is oaky with lots of pepper.

Real Hacienda Silver: Colorless, with a full, pungent attack. Moderate and *sencillo* agave intensity. White pepper and citrus dominate the nose, along with a bit of caramel. Sweet and full in the mouth, the tequila has astringent, earthy agave flavors. Ends with a short, hot finish.

Real Hacienda Reposado: Pale yellow color. Very little agave character, and what there is quickly succumbs to smoky, vegetal, beeswax aromas. These aromas carry over to the taste with the addition of cardboard flavors. The aftertaste is hot and abrupt.

Alteño Reposado: Yellow with brown edges. Attack is full and slightly pungent. Moderate agave intensity, but *sencillo* complexity. Some ginseng and floral aromas float around with a good hit of acetone. Slightly sweet with a medium mouth feel. Ginseng, dried flowers, and cardboard flavors. Long, hot finish with the cardboard flavors remaining dominant.

Xalixco
Lapiz
Pura Sangre
(NOM 1146)

In 1967 Roberto Orendain founded a small distillery called *La Tequileña* near the town of Tequila. Bacardi Corporation purchased the operation in 1981, rebuilt the facility and expanded operations. Bacardi introduced the Xalixco brand in the domestic Mexican market, but by 1987 had lost interest in tequila and decided to focus their attention on rum. Vergel Brandy from Mexico bought the plant, but continued to lose market share. In 1990, Vergel sold the operation to its present owner, Enrique Fonseca. Fonseca, one of the largest agave farmers in the state of Jalisco, reinvigorated the Xalixco brand. He added a 100% blue agave tequila called Pura Sangre, and he produces a third brand, Lapiz, for export to the United States.

The company uses a continuous action copper still for the first distillation, and a traditional copper alambic still for the second distillation. It produces close to 500 thousand liters of tequila annually. With Fonseca's agave fields, there are no worries about agave supply in the near future.

The house style is different from most, featuring a high acetone and smoky creosote character, which may result from the continuous action still. Lots of complex smoke and oak aromas and flavors compete with the agave flavors.

Tasting Notes

Pura Sangre Blanco: Colorless with a strong, pungent attack. Agave intensity is moderate and *suave*. Earthy agave aromas entwine with plenty of citrus and pepper, ending with a bit of honeysuckle. Sweet and thin in the mouth. Slight agave flavor with bits of sweet caramel quickly yield to a lip numbing, slightly bitter finish.

Xalixco Reposado: Pale yellow color with a full pungent attack. Moderate, *sencillo* agave intensity. Modest agave with lots of smoke, pepper, and creosote in the nose. Slightly sweet, but thin in the mouth. Smoky, doughy, cardboard flavors overpower hints of caramel. A smoky, bitter finish lasts quite a while and borders on lip numbing.

Lapiz Añejo: Light and mellow on the attack, this golden tequila exhibits moderate, *suave* agave complexity. Earthy agave and caramel dominate the aromas, but acetone elements also compete with pepper smells. Low sweetness with medium mouth feel. Caramel, earthy agave, and overripe apple flavors. Hot smoky finish builds to lip numbing levels.

Xalixco-Casta Añejo: Strong, pungent attack with *suave* complexity and *macho* intensity. ¡Ay caramba! caramel and high wet cement agave mingle with moderate fruit and spice aromas. Sweet with a medium mouth feel; the flavors are ¡ay caramba! cream soda with high agave and moderate pepper and oak. It finishes with medium sweetness, low bitterness, and cream soda flavor. The alcohol is tingly.

Other Tequila Brands and Producers

Arette Blanco: Made at a small distillery near the town of Tequila owned by a portion of the Orendain family, Arette Blanco is colorless with moderate candied agave aromas. Dry and astringent in the mouth, it has some earthy, dusty agave flavor that quickly fades into an astringent finish.

Casca Viejo Reposado: Another 100% agave tequila produced by La Arandina (along with Hipódromo), a medium-sized distillery in Los Altos, near Arandas. Pale yellow in color, with *macho* complexity, it has pepper and vanilla accents on full wet cement agave aromas. Moderately sweet and oily in the mouth, the wet cement agave and cream soda flavors provide a rich, smooth finish that trails off into a slightly doughy aftertaste.

Catador Añejo: This tiny producer, located in the Los Altos village of Jesus Maria, produces tequila with the typical wet cement character of Los Altos. Full and slightly pungent on attack, it is loaded with wet cement agave, smoke, and caramel. Sweet and thin in the mouth, the tequila features agave flavors with moderate smoke, caramel and pepper. The finish is sweet and tingly, of medium length, with cream and smoke flavors.

Hipódromo Reposado: This tequila is sold only in Mexico, and it is made by relatives of El Tesoro's Camarena family near Arandas. Pale yellow color. Light, mellow attack with *sencillo* complexity and moderate agave intensity. Wet cement agave with citrus, pepper and caramel aromas work well together, but in the mouth the flavors are muddled and confused. Sweet and salty on the finish.

Los Valientes Reposado: Another very small producer near the town of Tequila. Great packaging includes a canvas sheath glued to the bottle. The sheath features a printed photograph of *pistoleros*. The tequila is golden brown. Cream, toasty oak, and acetone fill the aroma. The slightly sweet mouth feel is much thinner than the nose leads you to expect. The flavors are redolent of toasty new oak barrels, and the aftertaste lasts a long, long time, but the flavor is nothing but toasty oak.

Tres Alegres Compadres Reposado: This is the 100% blue agave tequila made by La Cofradia distillery in Tequila, a medium-sized producer making about three million liters per year of *mixto* tequilas under various brand names. Pale yellow in color, with smooth caramel and hints of earthy agave in the nose, the tequila tastes astringent despite its medium body. The aftertaste turns to medicinal, smoky acetone flavors.

Tres Mujeres Reposado: This tiny new producer opened in 1996 just outside of Amatitan. The tequila is brown. Some earthy agave aromas are masked by vegetal and kerosene-like smells. Slightly sweet in the mouth, it quickly turns to smoky, burnt dough flavors that last well into the hot finish.

TEQUILAS BY STYLE

This chart rates the tequilas we tasted according to the intensity of agave flavor. If you find a tequila that you like, other tequilas in that same section will prove most similar. I hope this chart will help you choose tequilas that fit your flavor preferences. Brands in *Italic type* indicate sweet tequilas compared the rest of the class. Brands in **bold type** indicate oaky flavors compared to the rest of the class.

Light	Moderate	Macho	Muy Macho
Cuervo	Alteño	Aguila	Chinaco
Dos Reales	Arette	Casca Viejo	Patrón
San Matias	Cabrito	Catador	Siete Leguas
Torada	Cazadores	**Corralejo**	Tapatio
Tres Mujeres	El Viejito	Centinela	El Tesoro
Xalixco	Hipódromo	Cuervo Traditional	
	El Jimador	Don Julio	
	Los Valientes	El Amo de Aceves	
	Porfidio	El Charro	
	Pueblo Viejo	**Herradura**	
	Pura Sangre	Hussong's	
	Real Hacienda	Jalisciense	
	Sauza	Lapiz	
	Tres Alegres	Las Trancas	
		Regional	
		30-30	
		Tres Magueyes	
		Viuda de Romero	

PART III

THE TRAVEL GUIDE

CHAPTER 9

GOING TO MEXICO

If you love tequila, sooner or later, you have to go to Mexico and see the whole operation for yourself. Visiting the various tequila distilleries is an enchanting revelation. There is no describing the eerie, iridescent shimmer of blue agave fields stretching across the plateaus of Tequila or the rugged mountains of Los Altos. There is no better teacher of the blue agave life cycle than a walk through the fields with a grower and a chance to harvest your own agave with a razor sharp *coa de jima*. As you tour a distillery, the heavy, honeyed aromas of cooked, fermented, and distilled agave create an indescribable, intoxicating perfume that makes you giddy with the possibilities of the drink itself.

The tequila industry in Mexico is exploding. Rapid expansion, new tequila producers, continued interest, and expanding tourist amenities eventually will make touring tequila distilleries as popular as touring California wineries. My advice is to go now, before the whole enterprise becomes too tourist driven. Granted, you won't find much out there in the way of North American-style comfort, but the whole idea of tequila depends on its unique Mexicano sensibilities. If you have the adventurous spirit that leads you into the pleasures of tequila, you likely will enjoy the challenge that awaits you when you visit the distilleries.

Bear in mind that Mexico is, decidedly, a foreign country. Mexicano influences in the United States, especially in the Southwest, will not prepare you for life in Mexico. It may be our next-door neighbor, but the customs, language, and even the food are very different from ours. That said, Mexicanos are among the most hospitable of people, and they welcome tourists from the United States with a graciousness seldom seen in other foreign countries.

THIS IS NOT A TRAVEL BOOK

This section of the book is meant for a specific kind of traveler; the person going to Mexico to learn about tequila, who wants to visit some of the distilleries. It is not meant to be a generic travel book about Mexico, her people, her beaches, and her resorts.

For the tequila lover who wants to explore the tequila distilleries of Mexico, I will recommend my favorite places to stay and to eat. I will tell you what various distilleries offer in the way of tourist amenities, and I will give some basic information about how to get there. The rest is up to you.

I highly recommend consulting other, more generic travel guides for an overview of travel in Mexico. It will be helpful for you to have a broader vision of the culture and the country, and recommendations more directed to the general North American tourist. Here are two of my favorite travel guides to Mexico:

* *The People's Guide to Mexico*
  by Carl Franz (1992, John Muir
  Publications, 588 pages).

* *Travelers Guide to Mexico*
  by various authors (Published annually
  by Promociones de Mercados Turísticos,
  432 pages).

AT THE AIRPORT

If you are going to Mexico to learn about tequila, then you are going to Guadalajara. Guadalajara sits on a mile-high mountain plateau in the state of Jalisco.

One hour to the west by car lies the town of Tequila. Ninety minutes to the east stands Los Altos. These two areas produce 98% of Mexico's tequila.

You can drive to Guadalajara, but it is a very long way through some pretty amazing desert from whatever your point of origin. I recommend flying into Guadalajara's airport, Aeropuerto Internacional Miguel Hidalgo. You will land, taxi down the runway, and then descend onto the tarmac. Walk to the waiting buses, which will take you to the terminal, about 100 yards away. (It's a very short ride, but that's the way they do it.)

Inside the airport, you line up at customs. Show your passports and tourist cards (which are issued on the airplane), answer a few questions, and move on through. **Be sure to keep the copy of your stamped tourist card that you are given at this point.** You'll need it to leave the country.

Luggage usually arrives on the baggage carousel very quickly. There is only one carousel, so finding your luggage is easy, but you may have to fight your way through mobs of people to get your suitcase. Free luggage carts are available.

You walk about 20 feet to more officials who will take your Customs Declaration card (also issued on the airplane). Next to the officials, you will see stationary stoplights. You have to push the button on the stoplight. If it turns green, pass on through. If it turns red, the agents will check your luggage. No one knows exactly what they are looking for, but I don't advise taking drugs or firearms into Mexico. Twenty feet past the stoplights to your left is the exit. Poles prevent you from leaving with the luggage carts. Take your luggage off the carts and walk out the door to the curb.

Once you get outside, the taxi stand will be on your left. Go up to the window and tell the agent where you want to go. He will issue a ticket, and you will pay him about $10 US or 70 pesos, if you have them. Then go to the front of the line of taxis, hand the driver your ticket, tell him where you want to go, and get in. He will introduce you to the exciting world of driving in Mexico. Try to relax. Practice your Spanish. Ask the driver for the name of his favorite tequila.

When you get to your hotel, thank the driver, give him a 5–10% tip, and check in. Toss your bags on the bed, and then go straight to the bar for some tequila.

Welcome to Mexico.

EXCHANGING MONEY

The peso is Mexico's unit of currency. Since 1996, the peso has fluctuated between 7–8 pesos per US dollar. You can exchange cash or traveler's checks at banks, exchange houses (*casa de cambio*), hotels, restaurants, and shops. Banks give the best rates; hotels, restaurants and shops tend to give the worst.

Exchanging money in a Mexican bank is usually a time-consuming ordeal. It involves waiting in several different lines to get approval from various agents before you finally get in line to see a bank clerk and get your money. You can easily spend an hour exchanging money in a bank. Finally, banks will only exchange money between 10 A.M. and noon.

I recommend using the *casas de cambio*. They are authorized money exchange outlets, and their rates are only slightly lower than the banks. They are open from 9 A.M. to 7 P.M. with a two to three hour lunch break beginning at 2 P.M. An entire money exchange operation at a *casa de cambio* will take about five minutes.

When exchanging money, wherever you decide to do it, there should be a rate-of-exchange notice posted. If you don't see one, be sure to have the agent write the exchange rate on a piece of paper. The notice will look like this:

Tipo de cambio: 7.65
Venta: 7.90
Compra: 7.65

Tipo de cambio is the exchange rate for the day. *Venta* (sell) is the price you must pay to buy one US dollar. (This is the rate when you exchange your excess pesos back into US dollars.) Compra (buy) is the number of pesos they will pay for each US dollar you give them. If you exchange $100 US at a rate of 7.65, you'll get 765 pesos.

Credit cards, *tarjetas de crédito*, are widely accepted throughout Mexico at hotels, restaurants, and shops. We have found that using credit cards in Mexico often saves us money, because when we get home and receive our credit card bill, we usually notice that the credit card company has used a more advantageous exchange rate.

DRIVING IN MEXICO

I don't do it.

First of all, renting cars in Mexico is expensive. Then you have to worry about where to park the car, having it stolen, or having your stuff stolen from the car. Driving in Guadalajara is tricky. They have lots of traffic circles. They have one-way streets. They have crazy, maniacal, *macho* drivers who love to scare the hell out of you.

Taxis are plentiful. They are inexpensive. The drivers know where they are going. They will usually get you there safely. Negotiate the price of your cab ride before you get started. Generally, you can get anywhere in Guadalajara for 50 pesos or less ($7 US).

You can travel to the town of Tequila by bus. Once you're in Tequila you can hire taxis to take you to the various distilleries. The same is true for the towns of Los Altos. Personally, I prefer to use cabs to take me to and from the tequila districts. Then I use different local cabs to get to the individual distilleries. You can also hire a taxi for the entire day. This can be done for 400–700 pesos, or $50–90 US.

If you insist on renting a car and testing your mettle, all major rental agencies have offices in Mexico. It is always cheaper to make rental reservations from the United States than in Mexico. The problem with making the reservations from the United States is there's no way to guarantee the car you'll actually get in Mexico. Check with your insurance company to make sure you have proper coverage. Be sure to examine the car carefully for nicks, dents, and scratches. Mexican car rental agencies are notorious for charging for minor damages to their cars.

TRAVEL TRICKS

The first thing you should do when arriving at a new hotel is to pocket a card or brochure that carries the name and address of the hotel. That way, after a long day of sampling various tequilas, you can always hand it to a cab driver, and he will be able to get you home. It's easy to get lost in unfamiliar surroundings. Always have your hotel's address with you.

Carry a pencil and paper. When you ask for a price, whether for a taxi ride, a hotel room, or an item for purchase, have the seller write it down for you on the piece of paper. That way there is no misunderstanding due to language problems. You can still negotiate and bargain for prices, by simply passing the paper and pencil back and forth.

Study and learn our Basic Foreign Language Survival Phrases. These few easy-to-learn phrases are essential for surviving in any foreign country. Attempting to speak a foreign language may seem daunting, but it will endear you to the natives, and it's a polite show of respect for their country and culture.

BASIC FOREIGN LANGUAGE SURVIVAL PHRASES

Wherever we travel, we learn the following phrases in the native language. Proper grammar and pronunciation are not critical. It's the fact that you make the attempt to speak in their language that makes people want to help you. Mexicanos are an extremely polite people. You should always start any conversation with a greeting. Then, **no matter what you need to ask**, you should **proceed with the three survival phrases**. Only then should you ask your questions.

GREETINGS

English	Spanish (Pronunciation)
Good morning	*Buenos días*
	(bway-nohs dee-ahs)
Good afternoon	*Buenos tardes*
	(bway-nohs tar-dess)
Good evening	*Buenos noches*
	(bway-nohs no-chess)

SURVIVAL PHRASES

Excuse me, do you speak English?

> *¿Con permiso, habla usted inglés?*
>
> (Con pear-me-so, ah-blah oo-sted een-gles)

I'm sorry, I don't speak Spanish.

> *Lo siento, no hablo español.*
>
> (Low see-en-toe, no ah-blow ess-pan-yol)

Please, have patience.

> *Por favor, tiene paciencia.*
>
> Pour fah-vor, tee-yen-ay pah-see-en-see-ah)

QUESTIONS

Where is …	*¿Dónde está* … (Dohn-day ess-tah)
the bathroom	*el baño* (el bahn-yo)
the hotel	*el hotel* (el oh-tel)
a taxi	*un taxi* (oon tax-see)
the store	*la tienda* (lah tee-en-dah)
How much is …	*¿Cuanto es* … (Kwan-toe ess)
Do you have a …	*¿Tiene un/una* … (Tee-en-ay oon/oon-ah)
When?	*¿Cuándo* (kwahn-doe)
What?	*¿Mande?* or *¿Qué?* (Mahn-day or Keh)

Sᴛᴀᴛᴇᴍᴇɴᴛs

I don't understand.

No comprendo. (No comb-pren-doh)

I would like ...   *Quisiera* ... (Key-see-air-ah)

...a room   *un cuarto* (oon kwar-toe)

...the key   *la llave* (lah yah-veh)

...200 grams
(1/4 pound)   *doscientos gramos* (doe-see-en-tos gram-os)

Thank you.   *Gracias* (Grah-see-as)

You're welcome.   *De nada* (Deh nah-dah)

CHAPTER 10

DINING IN MEXICO

For Mexicanos, dining is a sacred ritual, and meals are savored slowly with long pauses between courses. Especially in Guadalajara, going to a restaurant is an event, and restaurants are jammed for both lunch and dinner. Lunch is often the big meal for Mexicanos, and they usually don't arrive at restaurants until 2:30 or 3:00. No Mexicano would ever consider making dinner reservations before 9:00 P.M., and most don't eat until 10:00 or 10:30. For the North American tourist, dining in Tequila country is likely to be the biggest surprise, for fine food of all types is available, with very good service, at remarkably inexpensive prices.

Dining in Mexicano restaurants is different than dining in the United States. First of all, being a waiter is a respected profession in Mexico, so waiters tend to have many years of experience and a long history of training at their jobs. Second, restaurants are not trying to "turn the table." Waiters never try to rush you through a meal, and customers are expected to linger at the table for several hours.

Typically, as soon as you are seated in a Mexicano restaurant, a waiter will approach the table and ask for drink orders. Far and away, the most popular beverages served to Mexicanos are soft drinks, but many people drink beer or cocktails. Wine is available only in the more upscale restaurants, with a limited and somewhat pricey selection.

Once the drink orders are taken, menus are brought to the table, often accompanied by a free tidbit, perhaps some small *empanadas,* or some soup, almost certainly some *salsa.* Your waiter will expect you to order a full meal consisting of several courses, and individual customers tend to eat what they've ordered. That is, Mexicanos don't share their plates with each other the way so many of us do here. If you want to try several dishes, and share them, simply tell your waiter. If he speaks English, or if you speak enough Spanish, he will gladly bring individual plates for each of you, and he will divide the dishes among you with a flourish.

Once the meal has begun, waiters will serve unobtrusively. You will find waiters most attentive. Especially in the finer restaurants, there are many plate changes, exchanging of silverware, and refilling of drinks. Take time to notice the little touches; the way the waiter brings ice and places it into your glass with silver tongs, or the tiny array of condiments served with a Mexicano soup dish. Expect lulls in between the courses. Because restaurants are in no hurry to turn the table, there is no rush to get you to your next course. Patrons converse, sip at their drinks, and observe the other people in the restaurants.

Upon completion of your meal, don't be surprised when you notice all your waiters have disappeared. In

Mexico, patrons often sit for hours after their meals without ordering anything. Waiters remove themselves, so as not to imply the need to rush. If you need a waiter to order something else, or to get the bill, a simple gesture to any waitstaff member passing by your table will quickly attract your waiter. Be aware that paying with credit cards is handled differently in Mexico. You give the waiter your card. He brings the receipt, you add the tip (10% is standard), sign, and then the waiter takes the receipt back to the owner, who only then will return your card. Pay attention, and don't leave the restaurant without your card.

Mexicano cuisine is much more varied than the *taco-burrito-fajitas* introduction we get in the United States. Seafood (*mariscos*) is very popular in Mexico, with certain restaurants dedicated to nothing else. Most *mariscos* restaurants are open for *comida* only, between 1–6 P.M. Different regions in Mexico are known for specific dishes, but all regional dishes are served throughout the country. Mexicanos love their meat, and most restaurants feature loads of beef, lamb, and pork dishes. While Mexicano dishes are always well-flavored with an array of spices, in general, they are not hot (*picante*) until you pour on the *salsas* served as separate accompaniments to the dishes.

As for international cuisine, Guadalajara has it all from Swiss to French, from Italian to Japanese. These international restaurants can be excellent, although familiar dishes tend to taste slightly different, especially those cuisines that use lots of sauces. The taste is due to differences in Mexicano butter, cheese, and cream. When used in sauces, or as cooking mediums, this indigenous flavor carries over to the dish. One thing for sure, whether it is Mexicano or international cuisine, tourists from the United States are likely to find the food salty. Be sure to taste your food before you add any salt.

Surprisingly, we rarely had a good cup of coffee in Mexico. As often as not, coffee in Mexico is instant coffee. Even restaurants serving espresso and cappuccino tend to make it on the weak side. The exceptions are the *"cafes"* in Atotonilco where boiling water is poured over whole, roasted coffee beans. This extracted coffee is so potent that it is served with a pot of hot water, so you can dilute it to your taste.

DINING VOCABULARY

Basics and Condiments are arranged in English and in alphabetical order, because you are more likely to need those without seeing them listed on a menu. All other items are listed in Spanish in alphabetical order, because you are more likely to encounter them in a menu.

BASICS		CONDIMENTS	
check	*cuenta*	butter	*mantequilla*
cup	*taza*	cheese	*queso*
fork	*tenedor*	garlic	*ajo*
glass	*vaso*	honey	*miel de abeja*
knife	*cuchillo*	jam	*mermelada*
menu	*carta/menu*	pepper	*pimienta*
napkin	*servieta*	salt	*sal*
on the side	*al lado*	sauce	*salsa*
plate	*platillo*	sugar	*azucar*
spoon	*cuchara*	oil	*aceite*
tip	*propina*	vinegar	*vinagre*
waiter	*mesero*		
wine list	*carta de vino*		

MEAT (CARNE)

barbacoa	barbecued goat	**jamón**	ham
biftec	beefsteak	**lengua**	tongue
borrego	lamb	**manitas de puerco**	pig's feet
cabrito	kid goat	**pancita**	tripe
carne molida	ground meat	**puerco**	pork
carne asada	grilled tenderloin strips	**res**	beef
carnitas	deep fried pork	**riñones**	kidneys
cerdo	pork	**rosbif**	roast beef
chicharrón	fried pork rind	**salchicha**	sausage
chorizo	spicy sausage	**sesos**	brains
chuleta	pork chop	**ternera**	veal
chuletas ahumadas	smoked pork chops	**tocino**	bacon
conejo	rabbit	**venado**	venison
costillas	spare ribs	**bien cocido**	well done
criadillas	bull testicles	**medio cocido**	medium
filete	tenderloin	**poco cocido**	rare
higado	liver		

POULTRY (AVES)

codorniz	quail	**pato**	duck
huevos	eggs	**pavo**	turkey
huevos fritos	fried eggs	**perdiz**	partridge
huevos revueltos	scrambled eggs	**pichón**	squab
huevos duros	hard boiled eggs	**pollo**	chicken
huevos tibios	soft boiled eggs		

SEAFOOD (MARISCOS)

abulón	abalone	**ostiones**	oysters
anchoas	anchovies	**pámpano**	pompano
almejas	clams	**pescado**	fish (caught)
ancas de rana	frog legs	**pescado blanco**	whitefish
anguila	eel	**pez**	fish (live)
atún	tuna	**pulpo**	octopus
bacalao	salted cod	**robalo**	sea bass
caguama	turtle	**salmón**	salmon
calamar	squid	**sardinas**	sardines
camaron	shrimp	**tiburón**	shark
caracoles	snails	**trucha**	trout
ceviche	marinated fish	**ahumado**	smoked
corvina	sea trout	**a la milanesa**	breaded
dorado	mahi mahi	**a las brasas**	charcoal grilled
escalopas	scallops	**a la parilla**	grilled
huachinango	red snapper	**al mojo de ajo**	garlic sauteed
jaiba	crab	**brocheta**	brochette
langostina	lobster	**empanizado**	breaded and fried
lenguado	sole	**frito**	fried
macarela	mackerel	**rostizado**	roasted
mojarra	perch	**veracruzana**	w/tomato and peppers

FRUITS (FRUTAS)

cerezas	cherries	**manzana**	apple
chabacanco	apricot	**mandarina**	tangerine
ciruela	plum	**melón**	cantaloupe
dátiles	dates	**membrillo**	quince
durazno	peach	**naranja**	orange
frambuesa	raspberry	**pera**	pear
fresa	strawberry	**piña**	pineapple
guayaba	guava	**sandía**	watermelon
higo	fig	**tuna**	prickly pear
limón	lime	**uva**	grape
mango	mango	**zarzamora**	blackberry

VEGETABLES (*LEGUMBRES*)

aceituna	olive	**esparragos**	asparagus
aguacate	avocado	**espinaca**	spinach
alcachofa	artichoke	**flor de calabaza**	squash flowers
apio	celery	**frijoles**	beans
arroz	rice	**jicama**	root vegetable
berro	watercress	**jitomate**	tomato (red)
betabel	beet	**lechuga**	lettuce
calabaza	squash	**nopales**	cactus leaves
camote	yam	**papas**	potatoes
cebolla	onion	**pepino**	cucumber
champiñones	mushrooms	**perejil**	parsley
chayote	mirliton	**pimiento verde**	bell pepper
col	cabbage	**rabanos**	radishes
coliflor	cauliflower	**tomatillo**	tomato (green husked)
ejotes	string beans	**zanahoria**	carrot
elotes	corn on the cob		
ensalada	salad		

Restaurants in Guadalajara

La Destileria

2916 Esq. Nelson at Av. Mexico

Phone: 640-34-40

Dinner/drinks per person: 100–140 pesos ($13–19 US)

Even if you don't like tequila, La Destileria is a trip. This "concept" restaurant owned by Grupo Orraca Restauranteros features regional Mexican food, a staggering selection of tequilas, and service that makes you dizzy.

The restaurant is located on Nelson at the corner of Av. Mexico, about six blocks from La Quinta Real Hotel. Car attendants, bus boys, and waiters are all dressed in color-coded uniforms to look like workers in a classy tequila distillery. Huge numbers of them buzz around your table, anticipating your every need.

The restaurant itself is a paean to tequila. The main dining room features red brick walls, high ceilings, and large windows. A large copper still dominates one corner, and classic photos with written histories of tequila distilleries adorn the walls. A full kitchen gleams in the center of the restaurant, where the chefs take great pleasure in flaming all sorts of items on their charcoal grills. Upstairs a loud bar thumps rock music, while young patrons sit around agave murals, *hornos* built into the walls, distillery equipment and displays of agave cultivation and harvest implements.

As soon as you are seated, hard-hatted distillery workers descend on your table bringing meat *empanadas*, *salsas*, limes, and a very salty shrimp broth in gorgeous ceramic shot glasses. Drink orders are a bit of a dilemma, since La Destileria features over 100 different tequilas listed by type (Blanco, Reposado, Añejo) and by town of origin. Just to give you an idea, the list for Reposado tequilas from Atotonilco includes Alteño, Don Julio, Las Trancas, Siete Leguas, Tres Magueyes, El Viejito, 30-30, and Jalisciense.

The extensive menu (also available in English with detailed descriptions of each dish) features food from all over Mexico. All the typical Mexicano dishes are available, including *tacos*, *quesadillas*, and steaks, but some wonderful, adventurous plates make the trip worthwhile.

A cold tostada featuring marinated octopus (*pulpo*) and strips of cactus (*nopales*) with guacamole was fabulous. Grilled items are a specialty, and the red snapper (*huacinango*) was done to simple perfection: moist, succulent, and redolent of charcoal flavors. Our favorite entrée was a *molcajete* of beef served sizzling in the traditional three-legged black stone bowl. In addition to the perfectly cooked strips of steak, the dish included cactus, whole green onions, cheese, and sausage all simmering in a delicious *chipotle* sauce. Soups are strongly flavored and on the salty side. *Quesadillas* are delicious, especially the one featuring squash flowers, corn mold (*cuitlacoche*), and mushrooms, but they come wrapped in a heavy, sometimes dry dough made from corn meal (*masa*).

It is customary to have an Añejo tequila after dinner. Ask for prices before you order, because these tequilas can get expensive. Desserts and coffee were available, but we couldn't pack in any more food. La Destileria is filled with young, hip Mexicano business people. They take their time, enjoy their meal and tequila, all the while in animated conversation. The food is good, sometimes extraordinary. The tequila selection and service are exemplary. The music is way too loud, but seems a small price to pay for what you get.

Trattoria Pomodoro

3051 Niños Heroes (2 blocks from Lopez Mateos)
Phone: 122-18-17
Dinner/drinks per person: 100–150 pesos ($12–20 US)

Michele Primucci is the classy proprietor of Trattoria Pomodoro. Originally from Basilicata in southern Italy, he spent 15 years in Toronto, and then moved to Mexico. In explanation, he says, "This is simple. I fell in love with a Mexican woman." All of Guadalajara owes this woman a debt of gratitude.

Primucci opened La Trattoria in 1976. He says it was slow going at first, but by 1980, La Trattoria was a local favorite. Today the restaurant serves 700 meals per day. The informal, casual atmosphere attracts a young, exuberant crowd. La Trattoria has 80 employees, and they are most attentive.

We sampled our way through most of the menu noting the Mexicano spelling of Italian dishes. The food is uniformly delicious. La Trattoria's strong point is their ability to serve simple, but perfectly flavored dishes.

Sauces are never overpowered by a single component; rather, they are delicious blends of flavors.

Fresh mussels (*mejillones*), farm raised in Ensenada, were served in a creamy broth tangy with garlic. *Carpaccio* had a rich but delicate flavor that rounded off the accompanying parmesan and olive oil. An antipasto bar featured mushrooms, eggplant, tomatoes, and mozzarella, and a delightful zucchini cooked with balsamic and red wine vinegars.

Of the entrées, *Scaloppine al Limone* was spectacular, featuring melt-in-your-mouth filet of beef (consistently good veal is difficult to get in Mexico) in a rich, tart lemon sauce. *Pollo ala Toscana* was made with remarkably tender chicken breast, sautéed with white wine, olive oil, rosemary, and a touch of lemon. A shrimp dish, *Camarones a la Diabla* was served in a cream sauce of white wine, chicken stock, and chiles. The rich sauce had a *picante* tang, although the frozen shrimp were a little tough.

La Trattoria has a wide range of pastas. *Pennette Cuatro Formaggi* made with parmesan, provolone, mozzarella, and Roquefort in a cream sauce was very good, but lacked that extra bite that puts this dish over the top. Better was the *Spaghetti alle Cozzi*, which paired delicious fresh mussels with a perfectly prepared olive oil-garlic sauce.

Of the several desserts, Primucci recommends the ubiquitous Tiramisu made without the unavailable mascarpone, but done well with cheese and cream in a layered cake soaked with sherry.

La Trattoria has a small, but good wine selection featuring Domecq wines from Mexico as their house wine, and includes Chianti, Valpolicella, Monte-pulciano, and Corvo. Michele buys what he can get, but laments that foreign wines are expensive, and distributors are often unable to maintain continuity. Wine prices range from 60–150 pesos ($8–20 US).

Service at La Trattoria is uniformly excellent. Attention is paid to detail; hot food is served on hot dishes, cold food on cold dishes. The restaurant provides an especially good bargain when you realize that all entrées include an extensive salad bar. The restaurant is open seven days a week from 1 P.M. to midnight. Ask to meet Michele, his son Alessandro, or Carlos the restaurant manager. They are truly charming people, and their restaurant is substantial proof that there is excellent Italian food in Guadalajara.

Itacates
Chapultepec Norte 110 (1 block from Av. Mexico)
Phone: 825-11-06
Dinner/drinks per person: 75 pesos ($10 US)

Itacates serves fine old style Mexican food. The original restaurant on Chapultepec features a long, narrow dining room. High-backed wooden chairs painted gaily in a profusion of pinks, blues, yellows, and greens are nevertheless terribly uncomfortable. Then again, you don't go to Itacates for comfort. You go to eat.

The food is traditional, terrific, and more than ample. *Botanas* include three *queso fundidos* (the great Mexicano version of fondue): plain, with *chorizo*, or with strips of *poblano* chiles. *Antojitos* are delicious, especially the rich *enchiladas* in *mole* sauce, and the tender *sopes* made with a choice of fillings. They offer freshly made *tacos* featuring your choice of 20 different fillings for a paltry three pesos each (40 cents).

Main courses include huge *chile rellenos* filled with cheese and vegetables, or *chiles en nogada*, chiles stuffed with meat in a walnut cream sauce topped with pomegranate seeds. *Pipian* chicken or pork is tender with a rich pumpkin seed-cumin sauce, much like a Mexicano curry. Pork in red chile sauce *(lomo adobado)* was well spiced, but a bit dry.

For the truly adventurous, Itacates serves *criadillas* (bull's testicles), either sautéed in a green sauce or deep fried. Everything comes with delicious, fresh tortillas. Half a dozen desserts, a dozen tequilas, and five rums make this a choice stop for the discerning diner.

Recco
Libertad 1981 (1/2 block from Chapultepec)
Phone: 825-07-24
Dinner/drinks per person: 135–160 pesos ($18–22 US)

Luigi Capurro took a circuitous route to Guadalajara. From his hometown of Recco, Italy, he went to England where he worked in the restaurant business. Somehow he wound up in Nepal, where, as hard as it may be to believe, he was told to try Mexico. He landed in Mexico City, and worked as a waiter and sommelier before moving to Guadalajara where he married a Mexicana. He opened Recco in 1973.

Recco has the feel of earlier times. Relaxed and beautifully set in an old home, it oozes Old World charm and formality. Juan Fonseca will likely greet you—he's been running the front of the house for 18 years.

We started with the *Paté de la Casa*, which was full-flavored, rich, and creamy with intriguing spices. It was served with glistening golden aspic and black olives, and was excellent when spread on Recco's signature grilled, toasted bread. Farm-raised mussels were exquisite in a light garlic broth. Forget the lime and hot sauce condiments that overpower the mussels, but be sure to sop up the broth with some bread like we did.

Mr. Capurro happily recommended the *Beef Bouillon Mexicana*, which started out as intensely rich beef flavors in a very salty broth. When you add the parsley, onion, chile pepper, and lime condiments, the soup is transformed into a bright, flavorful, palate-pleasing dish.

We sampled several pastas. A meaty lasagna with a sweet tomato sauce was good, but filling. The pasta Alfredo was well done, but Mexican butter and cream lend slightly different flavors than we are used to in the United States.

For entrées, *L'Arrosto* is a specialty of the house. Tender veal is rolled with garlic, wine, and rosemary, and then roasted served in a veal reduction sauce. Once again, Mr. Capurro set us up. He split the *L'Arrosto* among four of us, and then served us a green salad perfectly dressed with virgin olive oil and balsamic vinegar. "To refresh the palate," he said.

Then came another specialty, *Cacharro*, a pep-

TEQUILA COUNTRY

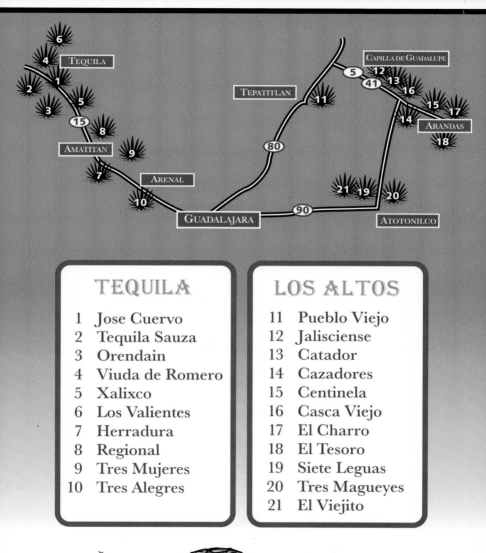

6
4 TEQUILA
1
2
5
3
15
8
AMATITAN
9
7
ARENAL
10
GUADALAJARA

CAPILLA DE GUADALUPE
5 12
41 13
11 16
15 17
14
ARANDAS
18

TEPATITLAN

80

21 19 20
ATOTONILCO

90

TEQUILA

1 Jose Cuervo
2 Tequila Sauza
3 Orendain
4 Viuda de Romero
5 Xalixco
6 Los Valientes
7 Herradura
8 Regional
9 Tres Mujeres
10 Tres Alegres

LOS ALTOS

11 Pueblo Viejo
12 Jalisciense
13 Catador
14 Cazadores
15 Centinela
16 Casca Viejo
17 El Charro
18 El Tesoro
19 Siete Leguas
20 Tres Magueyes
21 El Viejito

FROM AGAVE

Blue agave grows and matures for 7–10 years

Jimadores harvest agave

Reposado and Añejo tequilas are aged in oak

The finished tequila is bottled

Roasted agaves are milled
and mixed with water

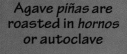 Agave *piñas* are
roasted in *hornos*
or autoclave

The *aguamiel* ferments in tanks

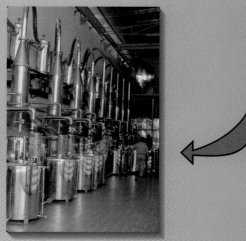

The *ordinario* is
distilled to
make tequila

After fermentation
the liquid is distilled
yielding *ordinario*

THE TEQUILA PYRAMID

A DESCRIPTIVE TOOL FOR THE TEQUILA AFICIONADO

Using The Tequila Pyramid is easy. The four outside steps of the pyramid categorize and then describe Aromas. Across the bottom are five flavors to assess, rated on an ascending scale from *Nada* to *¡Ay Caramba!* We also rate Sweetness and Bitterness on an ascending scale. Coming down the center steps, we rate Alcohol, Duration of Flavor and then give an overall rating.

pered beef filet served sizzling in a black iron skillet or
cacharro. The beef is cooked to perfection, wonderful-
ly tender, and seasoned with just the right amount of
black pepper. *Cacharro* is served with inch-wide
French fries and a side dish of steamed spinach with
cream. Recco also has a fine *Osso Bucco*, and serves
several sea bass dishes, including one made with dark
beer.

Desserts include caramel profiterole, a mild flan,
and an intense coffee-flavored tiramisu. Recco maintains one of Guadalajara's most extensive wine selections. A Chilean cabernet sauvignon imported by Jose
Cuervo, Clos San Jose 1992, was excellent and less
than $10 US. Recco is a place to relax and dine ele-
gantly course by course.

El Pargo del Pacifico

Av. La Paz 2140
Phone: 615-74-65 or 616-12-21
Dinner/drinks per person: 90–110 pesos ($12–15 US)

El Pargo is a simple, gorgeous delight. Bright and
airy, an indoor waterfall cascades quietly down the
back wall while fish tanks bubble in the corners. A wall
of windows in the front of the restaurant provides
unobstructed views of the dwarf palm trees. The
immaculate kitchen sparkles along the length of an
entire wall, and a tasteful mahogany bar fills in the
front corner.

El Pargo only serves *mariscos,* seafood. The basic
fish is red snapper. For 40 pesos ($5 US), you can have

your red snapper fried, steamed, sautéed in garlic butter, served *Veracruzana*-style with bell peppers, onions
and tomato, or *á la Diable* with chile.

Seafood cocktails run 17–42 pesos ($2.50–5.50
US), depending on size and ingredients. Salads featuring abalone, clams, shrimp, snails, or crab cost 30–40
pesos, ($4–6 US). Tostadas made with shrimp, crab, or
marlin *ceviche* cost 10 pesos ($1.25 US).

When you are seated, a waiter will bring a basket
of salty, toasted corn tortillas and a trio of hot sauces.
Be advised, El Pargo's *salsas* are not for the timid. The
green sauce is very tart with loads of lime juice, tomatillos, cilantro, and serrano peppers. It takes your breath
away. The red chile sauce is a fiery blend of dried chiles
roasted almost till burnt. Go easy or your tongue may
swell. The third *salsa* seems like a benign alternative,
but it is actually chopped pickled onions and *habanero*
chiles in a tangy vinaigrette. It will light you up.

Marlin empanadas arrive at the table steaming
hot, looking like sealed fried *tacos*. The fish is shredded
with various chiles and is very tasty with the corn tortillas, but the strong fish flavor of the marlin may not be
to your taste. *Flautas de Camaron* feature delicately
fried *masa* filled with a chopped shrimp stuffing. A few
drops of any of the hot sauces bring the appetizers to
sparkling life.

A wonderful soup called *Albondigas de Camaron*
fills a steaming bowl with delicate fish broth and several large shrimp dumplings. Delicious and delicate at the
same time, this is a classic example of Mexicano
seafood cookery at its finest.

One of El Pargo's specialties is the *Sarandeado* for

40 pesos ($5.50 US). A whole fish is filleted and placed skin side down over a charcoal grill. The fish is coated with a spicy red chile sauce. Both filets are served along with the center backbone (for people like us who love to munch the bones), slices of onion, cucumber, tomato, and avocado. The flavors from the charcoal grill and the chile sauce explode in your mouth, but don't overpower the rich flavor of the fish.

El Pargo is great fun and fantastic food. The restaurant attracts Mexicano business people wearing suits, ties, and cellular phones, but it's still a great place for a delightful, elegantly casual repast of fine seafood.

The restaurant features a decent selection of wines, both red and white, but it is hard to pass up your own personal miniature ice bucket full of 6-ounce bottles of *Pacifica de Sol* beer. A selection of coffee drinks and several fine tequilas are also available.

La Estancia Gaucho
Niños Heroes 2860
Phone: 122-65-65
Dinner/drinks per person: 90–140 pesos ($13–19 US)

La Estancia Gaucho has little charm, but it has great meat. You enter this Argentinian-style restaurant through a small courtyard that leads to a split-level dining room set with dark oak chairs and white linen tablecloths. A couple of potted trees, the bar, and a wine rack complete the scene. There you have it.

Most locals start with various *empanadas,* small fried dough pies filled with meat, cheese, potatoes, or vegetables. An order costs six pesos (about 80 cents US). *Empanadas* are served with La Estancia Gaucho's version of the classic *chimichurra* sauce—a rich, spicy garlic sauce made with parsley and chile—and the house red chile *salsa.* The long list of appetizers includes fried calamari, clams, and *lengua* (tongue). The unbattered *chiles rellenos* come lukewarm, filled with ground meat and cheese, and have a pleasant tart flavor. *Lengua vinagreta,* 53 pesos ($7 US), consists of remarkably tender slices of beef tongue covered with a tomato vinaigrette that contains tiny bits of chopped egg white. The dish was flavorful, but the vinaigrette overpowered the tongue.

When it's time for your steak, choices abound. La Estancia Gaucho uses Hereford beef exclusively imported from the United States. House specialties include *Churrasco,* a gorgeous hunk of sirloin in a 12-ounce size for $9 US, or a 17-ounce size for $12 US. The *Arrachera,* a long strip of skirt or flank steak, covers your plate like a side of beef. A full pound of T-bone sells for 55 pesos ($7 US). Filets range from $7–9 US depending on your choice of toppings: mushrooms, grilled onions, etc. All steaks are grilled, tender, and flavorful.

If you aren't thrilled with huge portions of beef, La Estancia Gaucho also serves fish, shrimp, and chicken. A rich rabbit stew and a flavorful veal shank are each priced at $7 US. All entrées come with a simple salad of iceberg lettuce and tomato. Desserts include banana pie, several ice creams, and a rich, dark flan swimming in caramel sauce and topped with chantilly cream. Coffee is good, and they offer espresso and cappuccino as well.

Open seven days a week, La Estancia Gaucho lists ten tequilas and offers 20 wines priced for 60–250 pesos, ($8–32 US) per bottle. Sunday afternoons are especially fun. The restaurant fills with large families, who cheer as they watch the local Mexican soccer team play its matches on a giant screen television.

Tierra
Av. La Paz 2235
Phone: 641-46-14
Dinner/drinks per person: 155 pesos ($20 US)

Tierra occupies a charming house painted a taste-challenging canary yellow. You can enjoy your meal and the mild Guadalajara climate in the large, lovely front yard patio. Inside the house, you may dine in one of three rooms. The smallest includes a full view of the busy kitchen of Chef Juan Pablo Rodriguez, a recent graduate of New York's Culinary Academy. The largest room has a wall of windows that open onto the patio. The third room is best for more intimate dining, or can be reserved for private parties.

The food at Tierra is innovative and challenging, and the presentations are elaborate. Appetizers included a corn blini with succulent smoked salmon in a tequila and chile vinaigrette. Their small pizza came topped with a puree of *jalapeño* chiles and slices of creamy goat cheese. Fried calamari with a Thai dipping sauce was disappointing—the sauce was too sweet and the calamari was slightly greasy. The duck terrine made up for this single glitch. Full of rich flavor, the terrine was served with a pear and port sauce. Appetizers range from 15–29 pesos, ($2–3.50 US). Three soups and three salads grace the menu. Soups include a cioppino and a gumbo. One salad features a peanut dressing, and another combines Roquefort and apples. Prices average $2.50 US.

Entrées are dazzling combinations of local Mexicano cookery and state-of-the-art creativity. Try the grilled rabbit prepared with *cilantro* oil and a purée of *habanero* chiles, accompanied by tart coleslaw and a fried egg roll. A blackened snapper rests alongside a purée of potato and baby onions. Chicken breast, stuffed with cheese and *chorizo*, comes with a mushroom Napoleon and a roasted shallot sauce. Chef Rodriguez perfectly balances the bold flavors and the bright chiles so that the chiles add to the flavors rather than dominate them. Main courses cost between $5–$10 U.S, and the wine list is short, at typical prices.

Hacienda del Bosque
Av. Paseo de las Arboledas 753
Phone: 121-85-28
Dinner/drinks per person: 100–130 pesos ($12–18 US)

Hacienda del Bosque is the quintessential Mexicano steak house, in a beautiful building in a quiet residential neighborhood. Hacienda del Bosque is a meat eater's paradise. Sure, the list of appetizers includes garlic mushrooms, *guacamole*, *empanadas*, and *ceviche* made from beef or chicken (if you dare), but you come to Hacienda del Bosque to eat meat, and the portions are large, so it's unwise to load up on too many appetizers.

Beef is the specialty of the house. *Cabrería* consists of thin strips of tender, delicious, marinated filet cooked over charcoal and then served on sizzling metal platters. You can order a kilo (2.2 pounds) for 140 pesos ($20 US). A smaller portion, a mere 550 grams (about 1.25 pounds) costs 99 pesos. *The Cañita del Bosque* is a spectacular single piece of filet mignon, weighing in at 300 grams (more than ten ounces). Incredibly tender with wonderful beef flavor, the whole dish served with a salad and French fries costs 50 pesos ($7 US).

As delicious as the beef is, one of our favorite dishes is *Borrego a la Parrilla*, a small mountain of tender charcoal-grilled lamb served with a bowl of rich lamb broth, red with spices. The idea is to season the broth to your taste, using the cilantro, chile, onion, and lime condiments, and then dip the lamb into the broth. The flavor is as unique as it is wonderful. *Borrego a la Parrilla* runs about $8 US, and will easily feed two people.

Hacienda del Bosque has three desserts: ice cream, flan, and pastries. As good as they are, customers are hard pressed to order one.

Service is excellent and professional. A small wine selection and a very good selection of tequila are available. Starting around 10 P.M., the restaurant features live mariachi music. All in all, an evening at Hacienda del Bosque provides a great meal, with wonderful entertainment.

Mariscos Progreso

Progreso No. 80

Tlaquepaque

Phone: 657-49-95

Dinner/drinks per person: 60–90 pesos ($8–12 US)

Mariscos Progreso is our favorite lunch spot in Tlaquepaque. Walk in before 2 P.M. and you'll be completely alone in the 200-seat courtyard. Start with a few cold beers or one of the dozen tequila offerings, and watch as people begin to stream in for lunch. Order a few tostadas to start. Ceviche, shrimp, or marlin are the choices, and they come simply, on hot crispy, salted corn tortillas for 5–10 pesos ($0.80–1.40 US).

By three o'clock the entire courtyard will be buzzing, every table full, with a line of people out the door munching on freshly shucked oysters from the outside cart. The smoky aroma of charcoal wafts through the courtyard from the open air mesquite grills in the corner, where chefs prepare four different types of fish, as well as gorgeous prawns wrapped in bacon. Grilled items cost 30–45 pesos ($4–6 US).

Leisurely order your way through the extensive menu. You can try the assorted platters featuring mussels, oysters, shrimp, and octopus for $5 US. Or you might prefer one of those classic Mexicano shrimp cocktails served in a giant chilled glass and topped with bits of guacamole and chile salsa 12–24 pesos ($1.80–3 US). For main courses, it's hard to resist the grill, but you can order trout, snapper, white fish, or many other fresh catches fried, baked, sautéed, or cooked in a variety of sauces. Prices are always between 30–45 pesos ($4–6 US).

While you're eating, pay attention to the strolling mariachi bands. Notice how many tables are seated with whole families—children, adults, and grandparents all enjoying a fine meal. Take note of the special service given to a group that purchases a full bottle of tequila. Realize that in Tlaquepaque, a town crawling with tourists, you are the only gringos in the whole restaurant. Then sit back and enjoy the interplay of Mexicanos having an afternoon out on the town.

Your entire meal, including appetizers, main course, drinks, and coffee will cost about $10 US per person. Reinvigorated, you can get in a few more hours of shopping when the stores reopen at five o'clock.

CHAPTER 11

HOME BASE: GUADALAJARA

Guadalajara is a beautiful city that continues to delight in spite of its exploding population. If you are visiting the tequila distilleries, Guadalajara will serve as your home base. Go downtown to visit the cathedral and the **Plaza Tapatia** comprising seven blocks of colonial architecture, sculpture, parks, fountains, and stores. There's a Tourism Office on the Plaza that provides maps and information.

Mercado Libertad, located at Calzada Independencia and Juarez is a must. Touted as the largest public market in the Western Hemisphere, the Mercado is bursting with color and personality. It's a raucous place with aggressive vendors coming at you from all angles trying to sell their wares. The crowded, high-energy market sells everything from food products and flowers to clothes and Mexican crafts. Sharpen your bargaining skills, and don't let the vendors intimidate you if you want to get any bargains. South of the Mercado at Obregon is the **Plaza de los Mariachis**. You can relax there after a hard day of shopping, and listen to *mariachis* while you have a few tequilas at the outside bar.

If you are looking for crafts, we have two places to recommend. **Casa de la Artesanias Jaliscense** is located in the Parque Agua Azul. It has a large assortment of crafts from the all over the state of Jalisco at fair prices. It's open from 10 A.M.–6 P.M. during the week, and closes a few hours earlier on Saturday and Sunday. The **Museo de Arte Huichol** has an exhibition of Huichol art featuring brightly colored bead work and string paintings. The Museo is in an annex of the Basilico de Zapopan. Zapopan is a suburb about 20 minutes from downtown Guadalajara. It is open from 10 A.M.–1 P.M. and from 4–7 P.M. during the week, and 10 A.M.–1 P.M. on weekends.

Tlaquepaque is a great place to spend a day, and it's just ten minutes from downtown Guadalajara. You will find some of Mexico's finest crafts interspersed amongst the tacky tourist shops. At the center of town is El Parian, a large plaza restaurant where you can relax with a drink and listen to musicians. There are several good restaurants in Tlaquepaque, but our favorites are **Mariscos Progresso** and **Fonda La Medina**.

Not far from Tlaquepaque is the town of **Tonala**. Tonala is known primarily for its ceramics and paper maché. Tonala is rustic, and doesn't have the fancy tourist character of Tlaquepaque, so we find it more relaxing. Try to avoid going on Thursday or Sunday when they have the huge outdoor market, unless you enjoy crowds, teeming streets, and lots of schlock for sale.

HOTELS IN GUADALAJARA

La Quinta Real
Av. Mexico 2727
Phone: 615-00-00
Fax: (3) 630-17-97
Rate for double room: 1,100–1,800 pesos ($160–$240 US)

Guadalajara is a major city, and it has several first-class hotels, but for my money, if you want to sit in the lap of luxury you go to La Quinta Real. La Quinta Real is the realized dream of Francisco Martinez Martinez. Although the hotel is only 11 years old, it appears gloriously ancient. Designed by famed architect Elias in a pre-Columbian style, the hotel wraps its massive stone walls around impeccably manicured gardens. A small shallow pool sits in a raised corner separated by a line of stone arches. Below the arches, tiered, natural fish ponds descend down to the gardens and the outdoor portion of the excellent restaurant.

All rooms at La Quinta Real are large, beautifully decorated suites. Some include whirlpool tubs. Rooms and interior corridors are loaded with Mexican art pieces. Rooms have honor bars, cable television, and free movies. La Quinta Real is an elegant, classic hotel. Prices are high by Mexicano standards, but far below North American prices for comparable digs.

Food in the restaurant is uniformly excellent from breakfast to dinner, with elegant and spectacular service. A prix fixe Sunday brunch for 42 pesos ($5.50 US) is a tour de force, and the slightly higher 46 peso prix fixe Sunday dinner is another marvel. Courtesy abounds from management to waitstaff to maid service.

In spite of its obvious luxury status, less than 20% of La Quinta Real's guests come from the United States. It provides a great peek into genuine Mexicano luxury. If you want to be truly extravagant, rent the Presidential suite, which includes three bedrooms, three baths, whirlpool tubs, living room, dining room and an enclosed patio. It rents for 4,500 pesos ($600 US) a night—not bad if shared by three couples.

Hotel Lafayette
Av. La Paz 2055
Phone: 615-02-52
Rate for double room: 350–450 pesos ($45–60 US)

I can't really explain what I like about the Hotel Lafayette. It's a standard kind of businessman's hotel. Two hundred rooms on seventeen stories with interior corridors. Two slow-moving elevators take you to and from your rooms. The staff is solicitous and helpful. It has a coffee shop, a restaurant, and a bar with a nightly happy hour that features live contemporary music.

The theme for the decor is blue. Blue carpets in the hallways lead to blue rooms. The fair-sized rooms usually have two queen beds, even if you've requested a single king. The rooms have a wheezing air conditioning system that is simply overwhelmed in the face of seriously high temperatures outside. Marble tiled bathrooms have combination bathtubs and showers. All rooms have cable television and free movies.

The Hotel Layfayette is basic. The rooms are clean and comfortable. There's plenty of space to store your clothes. There's a writing table and phone service. There's a small swimming pool just off the large main lobby area. The guests are an amalgamation of Mexicano and foreign businessmen, and a steady flow of international students. You'll hear conversations in dozens of different languages in the restaurants and lobby.

The best thing about the Hotel Lafayette is its location. Just two blocks south of the main intersection of Av. Vallarta and Av. Chapultepec, the hotel sits in a lovely residential section surrounded by a bustling business district. Centrally located between the downtown center of Guadalajara and the newer Plaza del Sol developments, it is close to **Los Arcos** and the **Minerva Circle**, (which delineate the end of old Guadalajara), and the Lazaro Cardenas Highway, which takes you to Tlaquepaque, Tonala, Chapala and the airport. Best of all, the Hotel Lafayette is centrally located to all of my favorite restaurants. You can walk to Tierra, Itacates, and Pargo. A short cab ride will get you to dozens more.

Holiday Inn Casa Grande

Aeropuerto Internacional Miguel Hidalgo
Phone: 678-90-00   Fax: 678-90-02
Rate for double room: 430 pesos ($62 US)

The Holiday Inn Casa Grande is one of our great secret finds. Located in Guadalajara's International Airport, it has 121 standard rooms and 27 luxury suites with Jacuzzi and steam baths. A swimming pool, workout room, and sauna are available. All rooms are soundproofed, and believe it or not, airplane noise is not a problem.

Rooms are spacious, new and immaculate, with tasteful decor and comfortable beds. There are chairs, a writing table, and a marble-tiled shower and bathroom with a separate wash basin area. The air conditioning works great, and there's plenty of hot water (although it takes a while for it to warm up). Free local phone calls. Free television with 13 channels. Free *U.S. Today* newspapers at the front desk.

And most importantly, the hotel offers free transportation to and from the city: a shuttle leaves the hotel every two hours from 10:00 A.M.–10:00 P.M. with service to Tlaquepaque, downtown Guadalajara, and the Plaza del Sol. We found the drivers entertaining and knowledgeable about restaurants and tourist sights. The shuttle will also return you to the hotel if you make reservations with the driver.

The hotel is very modern, with a huge indoor/outdoor bar. Guests receive two free complimentary drinks upon check-in. The nightly happy hour from 7:00–9:00 P.M. features two-for-one drinks for any national beverage (beer, tequila, or brandy).

Service is excellent, and everyone from bellhops to drivers to desk personnel speaks English. The hotel has a coffee shop with room service, but food is modest, at best.

The Holiday Inn Casa Grande is our hotel of choice for your last night in Guadalajara. You get a great room with terrific service and all amenities. You have a large room to do all your packing, and the bellhops will gladly take your luggage to the airport. From the hotel to the airport is a simple two-minute walk. There's no rush, no hassle, no wild taxicab drives.

CHAPTER 12

VISITING TEQUILA DISTILLERIES

As of 1997, very few tequila distillers offer much in the way of tourist amenities. Therefore, visiting distilleries is an adventure, and not for the faint at heart. The ability to speak Spanish, even rudimentary Spanish, makes things much easier, and will gain you great respect among the Mexicanos. Even when visiting the largest distilleries like Cuervo and Sauza, it is imperative that you make appointments in advance. (See Chapter 13: Contacting the Distilleries for more information and a list of phone numbers for the various distilleries.) For those of you interested in taking photographs, be aware that while portions of the distilleries are outside, much of the work is done in darker quarters. I have had good luck using high speed (400 ASA) film.

NEAR TEQUILA

About one hour northwest of Guadalajara by car or bus is the town of Tequila. Cuervo, Sauza, Orendain, and Viuda Romero are among the distilleries in Tequila. Herradura, Arette, El Gran Viejo, and Tres Mujeres are in nearby towns like Amatitan and Arenal. Sadly, neither Tequila nor any of the nearby towns offer much in the way of hotel accommodations or fine dining. When visiting Tequila, it is best to use Guadalajara as a base camp, and make day trips to the Tequila area.

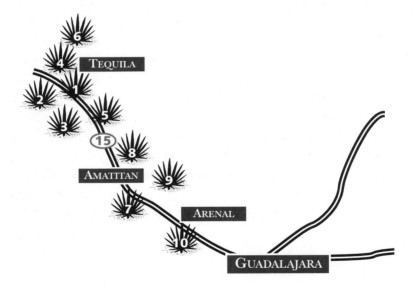

DISTILLERIES IN TEQUILA

Tequila Sauza   Sauza has a wonderful experimental agave plantation called *Rancho El Indio* not far from the distillery. You can see displays of the tools used to grow agave, take a walk into the plantation itself, and watch demonstrations of planting *hijuelos* and harvesting mature agaves in the fields.

After exploring the agave fields, you can taste all the Sauza tequilas, and then visit *La Perseverancia*, Sauza's distillery. Of particular interest is Sauza's practice of shredding the agave before cooking it in the autoclaves. Be sure to see the impressive Gabriel Flores mural. With enough advance notice, Sauza can provide an English speaking guide. Sauza also has a small sales office that sells a selected assortment of hats, shirts, and tequila.

Tequila Cuervo Jose Cuervo is the largest tequila producer in the world. The distillery, *La Rojeña*, is large, beautifully laid out, and tourist friendly. Murals and courtyards abound. Purple bougainvillea wraps around columns, setting off the stark buildings. Watching the workers split the agaves and load the *hornos* is interesting, and provides good photo opportunities. The distilling room with its gleaming copper stills is stunning. In spite of the scurrying workers and the vast amount of tequila being made, the feeling at *La Rojeña* is one of tranquillity.

Because Jose Cuervo is so big, it can offer varying levels of hospitality. Successful tequila sales people are treated to extravagant, entertainment-filled parties at the company *hacienda* across from the distillery. Regular tourists usually go on a simple tour with an English speaking guide, taste a few tequilas, and are sent on their way.

Herradura   Located in the town of Amatitan just a few miles south of Tequila, Herradura is in a class by itself. Far and away the most technologically advanced distillery in Mexico, Herradura sparkles with stainless steel tanks, pipes, and stills. As you enter the distillery, you will be greeted by banks of *hornos* in a continual state of being loaded with raw agaves, and then being unloaded with roasted agaves. Take note how ripe Herradura's agaves are in comparison to agaves from other producers in Tequila. Follow the agave as it travels from the *hornos* to the *moledor*, and from there through stainless steel pipes to the stainless steel fermenters. The distilling room shines in white-tiled splendor. Herradura is so modern and spotless that you can't help but be impressed.

Herradura also has a well-produced, although somewhat melodramatic video of the company's history. After watching the video, tourists are free to sample some tequilas and wander through the old historic distillery, now a museum. If you set it up in advance, you may be lucky enough to get a tour of the Herradura *hacienda* and gardens. With its glorious trees, pools, fountains, white peacocks, and other birds, it is a fitting paradise that matches the distillery. Only the sound of grinding gears from trucks laboring up the nearby hill disrupts the tranquility of the setting in a way that is uniquely Mexicano.

Viuda de Romero   This is a small distillery located right on the main highway in Tequila. Tourists are welcome to taste and buy the various tequilas in the tasting room. While small, the distillery has a certain charm. The long tubular autoclaves are different from the *hornos* at other distilleries. Seeing a distillery with a few stills, a small storage area, and a simple bottling line will give you a real feel for the primitive nature of much tequila production. Unfortunately, as of 1997, Viuda Romero had no English-speaking guides available.

Orendain   This is a large distillery that sits on a hill above the town of Tequila. Smaller than Cuervo or Sauza, and less technologically impressive than Herradura, Orendain is a good example of an efficient, day-to-day distiller of tequila. English-speaking guides are available with an advance appointment.

RESTAURANTS IN TEQUILA

As I have said, there is not much to recommend in Tequila in the way of fine dining. Nevertheless, if your schedule demands a lunch, I recommend **Mariscos El**

Mar, about one mile past Sauza's *Rancho El Indio*, just north of Tequila on Highway 15. The restaurant occupies a large outdoor pavilion with sweeping views of the canyons, agave fields, and mountains that surround Tequila. The view is magnificent.

Service is slow at Mariscos El Mar, so plan on a leisurely meal. The menu includes decent seafood and typical Mexicano dishes like *carne asada*. The beer is ice cold. Mariachi music is piped into the pavilion, and the bathrooms are clean. In short, it's a perfect place to have a cold beer, snack on some food, and take in the view. A full meal with drinks will run $4–5 US per person.

IN LOS ALTOS

The Los Altos tequila area is about one hour and thirty minutes to the east of Guadalajara. You can make it out and back in a day, if you limit your visit to one or two distilleries, but Los Altos offers enough decent accommodations for an overnight trip. Los Altos has several small tequila distilleries, located in three towns (Atotonilco, Arandas, and Tepatitlan), that form a triangle about an hour from each other.

ATOTONILCO EL ALTO

Directly to the east of Guadalajara is Atotonilco el Alto. It's a prosperous, genuine small Mexicano town with cobblestone streets, a pretty central plaza and a

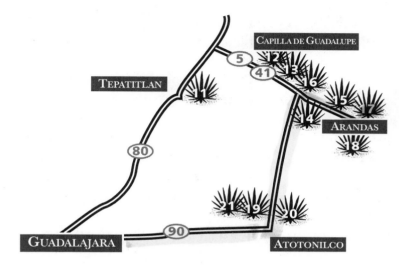

bustling mercado. You can get there taking the buses that depart hourly from Guadalajara's main station for 23 pesos ($3 US). A taxi ride will cost $300–400 pesos ($38–50 US) depending on your negotiating skills. Insist that the driver use the *Autopista*, a toll road that's much safer and quicker than the public road. It is well worth the extra cost.

STAYING IN ATOTONILCO

The place to stay in Atotonilco is **Portal de Vergel Hotel** at Andres Teran 45 (phone 391-7-19-13). The hotel opened in 1996, two blocks from the central plaza and across the street from the *mercado*. The clean, tiled rooms have a bath, a shower, and a fan. There is no air conditioning. A bar and restaurant opened sometime in 1997. Cost for a double room is 140 pesos ($19 US).

RESTAURANTS IN ATOTONILCO

The town features two decent restaurants. **Portofino**, directly on the central plaza, is upstairs and offers a bit of a view. **Navarra's Grill** on Avenida Independencia across from the *preparatorio* (high school) is very good. But for fine dining, head out of town about two miles on Highway 90 toward Mexico City. Chef Luis Navarro's **El Campestre Restaurant** serves some fabulous *comida* Mexicana.

Cucumbers and prickly pears sprinkled with lime and chile powder are complimentary starters. Two great roasted chile *salsas* grace the table, one made from *tomatillos,* the other from smoky *chile de arbol*. *Tostadas de nopales* (cactus) with *guacamole* are terrific, and so are the *sopes*, corn meal rolls topped with pork and spices dipped in a red chile sauce. *Enchiladas*, shrimp, and *fajitas*—El Campestre has it all, along with a beautiful view of the *barranca* (canyon) and the Sabina river.

Main courses include *cordoniz* (quail) marinated in lemon juice and then grilled. Loaded with tart lemon and smoky grilled flavors, the tender meat falls from the bone. *Borrego* (lamb) features a huge portion of nicely flavored lamb, but the meat was tough, dry, and overcooked. Entrées come with green salad, *fri-*

joles, and white rice with bits of chile and carrots. Beer is served in ice-cold mugs. There is a fine selection of tequilas, and the house lemonade is terrific. One caution: the portions are huge. A full meal will cost $5–9 US.

Another food stop to make in Atotonilco is **Panificadora Atotonilco,** a bakery on Av. Ramon Corona, three doors down from the corner at Av. Andres Teran (about two blocks from the Portal Vergel Hotel). You can choose from a wide assortment of *pan dulce* (sweet rolls), and some of the finest *bolillos* (rolls) in all of Mexico. Your first trip to a Mexican bakery can be a bit confusing. First, pick up one of the round trays and a pair of tongs, and then wander through the bakery, placing your selections onto the tray. When your tray is full, take it to the cash register, where they will package your purchases and charge you.

Believe me, the charge is minimal.

In Atotonilco, Tuesday is market day. If you are in town, visit the open-air street market that sets up between Av. Ignacio Zaragoza and Av. Pedro Valle Navarro about two blocks from the square, and meander through the myriad of stalls. While there may not be much of artistic merit, it's a perfect opportunity to see the weekly workings of a Mexicano market.

DISTILLERIES IN ATOTONILCO

El Viejito   This medium-sized producer makes dozens of different tequilas including El Viejito, Hussong's, Don Quixote, Los Cinco Soles, and Distinct (flavored tequilas). They also make tequila in a joint venture for Aguila. Close to 90% of the production is exported to other countries. The distillery is just a few blocks from the center of town. It is small and compact with both autoclaves and a few *hornos*. Owner Antonio Nuñez speaks English as does his family. They are pleasant, charming people who will offer a simple tour of the facilities if you set up an appointment.

🌵**Siete Leguas**   This is the original producer of the famous Patrón tequila, so loved in the United States. Owner Lucretia Gonzales does not sell her Siete Leguas brand tequila in the United States. Two separate distilleries are nestled within a block of each other midway up the steep Calle 16 de Septiembre. Generally, no tours of the actual distillery are offered, but Siete Leguas has a tasting room and sales shop just outside of Atotonilco at the intersection of the road to Arandas.

🌵**Tres Magueyes**   Eduardo Gonzales (Lucretia's brother) owns Tres Magueyes, which produces the well-known Don Julio brand. Simple, clean, and compact, Tres Magueyes is the quintessential, midsized tequila distillery. There is a small barrel storage facility on site, but the bulk of their six thousand barrels is stored in another facility. Tres Magueyes is also difficult to visit, but late in 1996 Rémy Martin obtained rights to sell Tres Magueyes tequilas, including Don Julio, outside of Mexico. One can only hope that the Rémy Martin people will convince Eduardo to provide some tours of the distillery.

ARANDAS

Flecha Amarilla buses leave from Atotonilco for Arandas five times a day between 6:30 A.M. and 5:30 P.M. The 40-minute ride costs 11 pesos ($1.50 US). A taxi ride to Arandas costs 100 pesos ($13 US). I recommend taking a cab. Ask the driver to take the old road past the Siete Leguas distilleries.

The drive out of Atotonilco to Arandas is one of the most spectacular in all of tequila country. A steady climb out of town takes you through agave fields that cling to the steep mountainsides. As you leave Atotonilco, the steel-blue ribbons of agave flow down the mountains at dizzying angles. The blue agave plants tenaciously grip the earth and fight the weeds for sustenance. All you need to know about the magic of tequila is visible in these treacherous fields above Atotonilco. From the peak, you look back on a breathtaking view of Atotonilco with its gold roofed cathedral, and the long, wide valley stretching for miles beyond the town. The rest of the short ride to Arandas pales in comparison.

Arandas is a small, dusty town with a large cathedral modeled after the one in Lourdes. The town square is a few blocks from the cathedral. For its size, Arandas is a treasure trove of fine tequila: El Tesoro (Tapatio), Centinela (Cabrito), Cazadores, and El Charro are all located in the town of Arandas.

STAYING IN ARANDAS

Staying in Arandas used to be simple. There was only one hotel to consider. Built in 1995, **El Castillo de Cristal**, located across the street from the cathedral on the main street through town, provides a double room for 125–140 pesos per night ($18–20 US). The phone number is (378) 3-05-20. Shaped like a castle and completely covered with mirrors, it must be seen to be believed. Rooms are clean but noisy due to the interior courtyard configuration. Furniture is inexpensive, and may deteriorate rapidly. In any case, there are no other adequate choices in Arandas. Fortunately, the owners of Cazadores Tequila are constructing a new hotel just three blocks from the cathedral. Scheduled to open late 1997, it will doubtless become the place for visitors in Arandas.

RESTAURANTS IN ARANDAS

I think the best restaurant in Arandas is **La Terraza**, about one mile north of town on the main highway. It features *comida* Mexicana. Fifteen beef dishes, six pork, five chicken, and two seafood dishes grace the menu. All run between 22–28 pesos ($3–4 US). They have a wonderful *picante guacamole* made with pumpkin seeds. Giant ham hocks, slow-baked in *adobe* ovens with a red chile sauce, were delicious. *Carne asada*, *moles*, *empanadas*, *tacos*, and *enchiladas* are all available. An entire meal is about $6 US.

On the Plaza, **Restaurant Penita** has the best coffee in town, and is a good place for breakfast. For an adventurous, remarkably inexpensive meal, try **El Dorado** on Av. Juarez, just off the plaza, behind the church. El Dorado sells *tacos al pastor* for one peso each, about 15 cents US.

   The truly adventurous among you should try **Cenaduria "Rosy"** at Constituyentes and Colon (about two blocks from the cathedral.) Cenaduria "Rosy" is everything you've ever been warned against in Mexico; a tiny room painted blue with five blue metal tables and matching blue chairs. The walls, the ceiling, and the floor are painted blue. All the sauces are red, and Rosy serves the best *pozole* (a meat soup made with hominy) that you've ever tasted. Open from 8–11:30 P.M., a full meal at Rosy's will cost no more than 23 pesos ($3 US). By the way, if the local Aguilas Negras Mariachi band is playing in town, look for Rosy's father who is one of the members.

DISTILLERIES IN ARANDAS

Cazadores   Cazadores is a new, very successful, state-of-the-art facility just   north of Arandas. With advance notice, they will arrange for an English-speaking tour guide. The plant is spotless, large, and busy with activity. Autoclaves are used instead of *hornos*, and classical music plays to soothe the fermenting agave. The focus is on Reposado tequila, aged in new oak barrels. The immediate and tremendous success of Cazadores in Mexico contributed to the great surge in Mexican consumption of Reposado tequilas. A new tasting room and restaurant were scheduled to open in 1997.

🌵**Centinela**   Centinela is one of the two grand old tequila producers of Arandas. The *fábrica* is about two miles north of Arandas, just off the main highway. The *fábrica* itself seems to be bursting at the seams with a haphazard sort of expansion. From 1995 to 1997, Centinela increased production from three to fifteen thousand liters a day. *Hornos* are crammed into the central grounds. Fermentation tanks are jammed together and connected with rickety walkways. Stills of every type and shape fill the small distilling room, and every *adobe* shed on the property is bursting with storage barrels. Tours can be set up at the Centinela office on the main plaza in Arandas, but we've never met anyone there or at the *fábrica* who speaks English.

🌵**El Tesoro**   The offices, bottling plant, and aging facility for El Tesoro (also known as Tapatio in Mexico) are located on the main street just across from the main plaza. El Tesoro is the other grand old tequila producer of Arandas. English tours are available with advance notice. Their famous distillery, *La Alteña*, is about three miles south of town, down dusty, bumpy, winding dirt roads. A visit is well worth the discomfort of getting there.

As of this writing, El Tesoro is in the midst of a giant new construction project building modern, new production facilities. In the meantime, *La Alteña* uses *hornos,* a working *tahona*, and men carrying crushed agave on their heads in wooden buckets. The juice ferments in wooden tanks with a *batidor* (a man who separates the agave pulp by hand) inside. The fermented juice is again carried by bucket to the stills. Incredibly educational in an ancient, prehistoric way, *La Alteña* is not to be missed by any true tequila enthusiast.

El Charro   This is the newest tequila factory in Arandas, about two miles south of town. It's small, new, and appreciated by all the locals. For a tour, walk into their new tasting room on the town square and ask for the owner, Javier Lopez Orozco. Javier doesn't speak English, but he's very enthusiastic and loves to show off his *fábrica*.

The distillery itself is ultra modern, with a unique machine that splits the agave *piñas* while removing the tasteless core. Director Arturo Fuentes, with more than 20 years experience making fine spirits, has developed a scientific methodology to produce El Charro. Arturo is an eloquent spokesperson for progressive tequila production techniques.

TEPATITLAN

Flecha Amarilla buses leave every 30 minutes from the bus station in Arandas headed for Tepatitlan. The ride takes 75 minutes and costs 14 pesos ($2 US). The buses fill with school children and locals going about their business, and offer some insight into daily Mexicano culture. Taking a taxi from Arandas to Tepatitlan costs 180 pesos ($28 US) and cuts the travel time down to a little less than an hour.

Several bus lines provide service between Tepatitlan and Guadalajara. Buses leave every 30 minutes. Taxi prices from Tepa to Guadalajara range from

250 pesos ($32 US) for a hair-raising ride on the public roads to 300 pesos ($38 US) for a much more relaxed return on the *Autopista*. Locals affectionately refer to Tepatitlan as "Tepa," and it is a favorite day trip for Guadalajara residents. A gorgeous cathedral dominates a pretty and clean double plaza in the center of town. A dozen hotels can be found within a block of the central plaza with prices ranging between $20–$40 US.

If you visit Tepa in the last two weeks of April, you are sure to encounter the *Feria de Tepa* (Tepa Holiday), which fills up the central plaza with thousands of people for a fortnight. A spectacular 20 minutes of fireworks light up the sky each night. Mexicano fireworks are something to behold. Rickety bamboo towers flame, and take off screaming amidst showers of sparks until the rockets explode high in the sky above the crowd. More than 100 different *mariachi* groups and *bandas* vie for the attention of the revelers. Dozens of tequila manufacturers set up sampling booths. The party and the music go on night after night, well into the morning. At dawn the eight local churches set off dozens of cannon rounds to wake up the revelers and call them to church for atonement.

RESTAURANTS IN TEPATITLAN

For fine dining in Tepa, we like **El Vitral** on the corner of Av. Hidalgo and Vincente Guerrero, just two blocks from the central plaza. Housed in an historic cool green hacienda with 16-foot ceilings and sturdy carved wooden shutters, El Vitral defines casual elegance.

Typical appetizers include a creamy *guacamole* loaded with lime, spicy with *serrano* chiles, and seasoned with bits of tomato and onion. *Nachos, quesadillas,* and *chicharrones* (fried pork rinds) in red sauce fill out the list. Entrées tend toward beef, with 15 choices priced between 35–40 pesos ($5–6 US), or shrimp, with 10 choices at 45 pesos ($6 US). A good choice was the *Brochette de filete,* tender chunks of marinated filet that's first grilled, and then sautéed with bacon, bell pepper, onion, and apple. It comes with baked potato, rice and green salad. Also on the menu are a few fish, chicken, and pork dishes. The *Lomo adobado de la casa* turned out to be a huge, thin strip of pork served with a perfect, rich red chile sauce. The accompanying *guacamole* worked beautifully with the spicy pork. Entire meals with appetizer, entrée, and drinks run about 75 pesos ($10 US) per person. As usual, with fine Mexicano restaurants, service is wonderfully professional.

On a much more informal side, Tepa is renowned for its *carnitas*—slow cooked pork that is chopped up and served with tortillas in soft *tacos.* There is continual debate over which restaurant serves the best *carnitas.* In truth, it's hard to go wrong. Most restaurants sell *carnitas* by the kilo for about 50 pesos (that's $7 US for more than two pounds of meat).

A final note about dining in Tepa. Located directly on the main plaza at Niños Heroes No. 51 is a small pizzeria called **Pizza Togo**. On two separate occasions, during two completely different trips, we have had the best French fries in all of Mexico here. Give it a try, but be patient, because they are made to order.

Distilleries in Tepatitlan

🌵**Pueblo Viejo, San Matias**   This factory, known locally as *Ojo de Agua de Latillas* (Eye of Tears), produces the 100% agave Pueblo Viejo as well as the *mixto* San Matias. More than 90% of the production is sold in Mexico, and Pueblo Viejo has a great reputation as a fine tequila in Mexico. It is definitely the overwhelming favorite of cab drivers in Guadalajara.

🌵**30-30, Jalisciense**   This tequila distillery is about two miles from the town of Capilla de Guadalupe, which is halfway between Arandas and Tepatitlan. Under the direction of Elpidio Aceves this new distillery hopes to expand. Elpidio's brother Javier markets his own brands, Jalisciense and El Amo Aceves. Both Elpidio and Javier speak fluent English, and will be happy to guide you through the distillery if you make an appointment.

CHAPTER 13

CONTACTING THE DISTILLERIES

If your adventurous spirit demands that you visit the various tequila companies, the first step is to set up an appointment. Most tequila distilleries maintain offices in Guadalajara. Their phone numbers change frequently, but can be found in the yellow pages under Tequila. Unfortunately, in most cases they are listed under their company names, not their brand names.

In this section, I have listed most of the major tequila brand names, followed by the company names, addresses, and phone numbers. Call them, ask for someone who speaks English, and then try to set up a tour. If they are reluctant, tell them what they want to hear—that you are a writer or a buyer for a restaurant or store in the United States.

Be advised, even a firm appointment on a specified date at a designated time is no assurance that anyone will know you are coming. Sometimes, just knocking at the door of a distillery can set you up for a great tour. Of course, speaking Spanish sure helps.

New distilleries and tequila brands pop up quicker than *hijuelitos* from a mature agave plant. As of

January 1, 1998, there were 46 licensed, operating distilleries producing more than 300 different brands of tequila, with 13 new distilleries expected to open thereafter. I have concentrated on the most popular brands, and those most likely to be found in the United States. (See the list of tequilas arranged by location at the end of this chapter.)

ARETTE

Tequila Parreñita
Av. Alcalde No. 859
Guadalajara, Mexico
Phone/fax (523) 613-6078

No tours, no tasting, no help.

CAZADORES

Tequila Cazadores
Km. 3 Libramiento Sur
Arandas, Jalisco, Mexico
Phone (523) 784-5570
Fax (523) 784-5189

Beautiful facility. State of the art production. Tours by appointment. English tour possible. Plans include restaurant and tasting bar. Hotel open in nearby Arandas.

CENTINELA

Tequila Centinela
Av. Francisco Mora No. 8
Arandas, Jalisco, Mexico
Phone (523) 783-0468
Fax (523) 783-0933

Tours by appointment only. No English tours as of January 1998. Aggressive, excellent tequila maker bursting at the seams with expansion.

EL CHARRO

Tequilera Rustica de Arandas
Norberto Gomez No. 408
Aguascalientes, Mexico
Phone/fax (524) 916-1046

New, small, state of the art distillery. Beautiful grounds. Tours possible, but not yet in English. Tasting room in Arandas on main square.

CHINACO

Tequilera Gonzáleña
Gonzáles, Taumalipas, Mexico
U.S. Phone (810) 229-0600

In northern Mexico, south of
El Paso Texas.

CORRALEJO

Tequilera Corralejo
Estacíon Corralejo
Pénjamo, Guanajuato, Mexico
Phone (524) 977-0203
Fax (524) 877-0334

Open Monday through Friday from
8 a.m. to 5 p.m., and Saturday from
8 a.m. to 2 p.m. Tours and tasting
daily at the historical Hacienda
Corralejo.

CUERVO

Tequila Cuervo La Rojeña
Circunvalción Sur,
No. 44-A Las Puentes
Zapopan, Jalisco, Mexico
Phone (523) 634-4298
Fax (523) 634-8893

Classic, giant distillery in center of
Tequila. English tours available by
appointment. Tasting available. Gift
shop.

HERRADURA

Tequila Herradura
Av. 16 de Septiembre No. 635
Guadalajara, Jalisco, Mexico
Phone (523) 614-0400
Fax (523) 613-1698

The modern factory to see, if you
can only see one. English tours by
appointment. Beautiful grounds,
stunning distillery, historical video
and tasting.

HIPÓDROMO

La Arandina
Periferico Norte Lateral Sur No. 762
Zapopan, Jalisco, Mexico
Phone (523) 636-2430
Fax (523) 656-2176

Small producer in Arandas. Cousins
to the Camarenas of El Tesoro.
Difficult to contact. Few amenities.

JALISCIENSE

Agroindustrias Guadalajara
Rancho El Herradero No. 100
Capilla de Guadalupe,
Jalisco, Mexico
Phone (523) 712-1515
Fax (523) 712-1331

English tours available by
appointment. Adventurous ride
out of town. Modern facility,
possible tasting.

LOS VALIENTES

Industrialización y Dllo.
Santo Tomas Niñoz
Heroes No. 1976
Guadalajara, Mexico
Phone (523) 826-4881

Small producer near the town of
Tequila. Located in an old historical
hacienda.

MONTEZUMA

Distiladora González González or
Destiladora de Occidente
Hidalgo No. 829
Guadalajara, Mexico
Phone (523) 742-0100

Modern, scientific approach to
making tequila. Located in the
city of Guadalajara. English tours
available with appointment.

ORENDAIN

Tequila Orendain de Jalisco
Av. Vallarta No. 6230
Zapopan, Jalisco, Mexico
Phone (523) 627-1827
Fax (523) 627-1376

Large producer located above the
town of Tequila. Simple, modern
facility with no frills. Tours available
with appointment. No tasting.

PUEBLO VIEJO

Tequila San Matias de Jalisco
J.J. González Gallo No. 2565
Guadalajara, Mexico
Phone (523) 635-2046
Fax (523) 635-8780

A large distillery located in
Tepatitlan. Tours and tastings
up in the air, due to the murder
of Jesus Lopez.

REGIONAL

Empresa Ejidal Tequilera Amatitan
Cam. a la Barranca de Tecuane S/N
Amatitán, Jalisco, Mexico
Phone (523) 745-0043

Small co-operative producer across
the street from Herradura. Hard to
get into, but persistence might get
you a tour.

RIO DE PLATA

Tequilas del Señor
Rio Tuito No. 1193
Guadalajara, Mexico
Phone (523) 657-7787
Fax (523) 657-2936

Another large distiller located in
Guadalajara. English tours available
with appointment.

SAUZA

Tequila Sauza
Av. Vallarta No. 3273
Guadalajara, Mexico
Phone (523) 679-0600
Fax (523) 679-0690

One of the most educational tours
in the business. English guides
available with appointment. Tour
includes visit to experimental agave
field and full tasting. Gift shop.

SIETE LEGUAS

Tequila Siete Leguas
Av. Independencia No. 360
Atotonilco el Alto, Jalisco, Mexico
Phone (523) 917-0996
Fax (523) 917-1891

Even with an appointment, it's
almost impossible to get into this
distillery. Tasting room open in
Atotonilco. You might get in if
you show up unannounced at the
distillery.

EL TESORO

Tequila Tapatio
Alvaro Obregón No. 35
Arandas, Jalisco, Mexico
Phone (523) 783-0425
Fax (523) 783-1666

A must-see distillery exhibiting
ancient tequila making methodology.
English tours and tasting available
with advance reservation. Allow
at least half a day.

TRES ALEGRES COMPADRES

La Cofradia
Mariano Barcenas No. 435
Sector Hidalgo
Guadalajara, Mexico
Phone (523) 613-6690
Fax (523) 613-6641

Mid-size distillery located in the
town of tequila. Tours available with
appointment.

EL VIEJITO

Tequila El Viejito
Eucalipto No. 2234
Guadalajara, Mexico
Phone (523) 812-9092
Fax (523) 812-9590

Tours available by appointment
only. Owners and some personnel
speak English. Bottling plant is in
Guadalajara. Distillery is in
Atotonilco.

XALIXCO

Tequileña
Bruselas No. 285
Guadalajara, Mexico
Phone (523) 826-8070
Fax (523) 827-0249

Tours available by appointment.
Check out continuous action still used
to make ordinario. Traditional still
for second distillation.

TEQUILAS BY LOCATION

AMATITAN
Herradura
El Jimador
Regional

ARANDAS
Cabrito
Casco Viejo
Cava de Don Agustin
Cazadores
Centinela
Dos Amigos
El Charro
Hipódromo
Tapatío
El Tesoro

ATOTONILCO
Alteño
Don Julio
Hussong's
J. R.
Lapiz
Siete Leguas
Tres Magueyes
El Viejito

CAPILLA DE GUADALUPE
30-30
Ambarfino
El Amo Aceves
Jalisciense
Las Trancas

TAMAULIPAS
Chinaco

GUADALAJARA
Catador
Caballito Cerrero
Diligencia
Herradura del Señor
Mayor
Porfidio
Sombrero Negro
Los Valientes

TEPATITLAN
Pueblo Viejo
San Matias

PÉNJAMO
Corralejo

TEQUILA

Alteño
Arette
Centenario
Chamucos
Dos Reales
José Cuervo
Los Valientes
Ollitas
Orendain
Pura Sangre
Real Hacienda
Sauza
Tequileño
Tres Alegres
Tres Mujeres
Virreyes
Viuda de Romero
Xalixco

FINDING SECONDARY BRAND NAMES

In this section I have listed secondary tequila brands produced at the distilleries listed above. Find the tequila brand in which you are interested, and this list will guide you to the actual producer.

AGUILA (El Viejito)

ALTEÑO (Viuda de Romero)

CABRITO (Centinela)

CENTENARIO (Cuervo)

CONMEMORATIVO (Sauza)

COYOTE (Orendain)

DILIGENCIAS (Rio de Plata)

DISTINCT (El Viejito)

DON JULIO (Tres Maguyes)

DON QUIXOTE (El Viejito)

DOS REALES (Cuervo)

EL AMO ACEVES (Jalisciense)

EL JIMADOR (Herradura)

GALARDON (Sauza)

GIRO (Sauza)

HACIENDA DE TEPA (El Charro)

HORNITOS (Sauza)

HUSSONG'S (El Viejito)

JOSE CUERVO (Cuervo)

JUAREZ (Montezuma)

LAPIZ (Xalixco)

LAS TRANCAS (Jalisciense)

OLLITAS (Orendain)

PATRÓN (Siete Leguas)

PEPE LOPEZ (Orendain)

PORFIDIO (multiple producers)

REAL HACIENDA (Viuda de Romero)
RESERVA DE LA FAMILIA (Cuervo)
SAN MATIAS (Pueblo Viejo)
SIERRA (El Viejito)   *GERMANY'S #1*
TAPATIO (El Tesoro)
TORADA (Rio de Plata)
TRES CABALLOS (El Charro)
TRES GENERACIONES (Sauza)

GLOSSARY OF TEQUILA TERMS

Abocado	Unaged tequila to which coloring and flavoring have been added.
Agave azul	The specified variety of *maguey* from which tequila is made.
Aguamiel	The unfermented juice extracted from the roasted agave.
Añejo	Tequila that has been aged in oak barrels for at least one year.
Autoclave	A large pressure cooker used to cook the agave *piñas*.
Bacanora	A distilled drink made in Sonora from *maguey*, but not from blue agave.
Barrica	Barrel
Batidor	The worker who separates agave fiber from *aguamiel* as it is dumped into a tank.
Blanco	Colorless, unaged tequila.
Cabeza	The first portion of distillate, highest in alcohol and aldehydes, which is usually discarded.

Coa de jima	A specialized tool used for harvesting agave.
Colas	The final portion of distillate containing the lowest alcohol and soapy flavors, usually recycled into another distillation.
Corazón	The "heart" of a distillation containing the best flavors and aromas for tequila.
Fábrica	A tequila distillery.
Hijuelo	A "baby" agave plant cut from the "mother" and replanted to develop into a mature agave plant.
Horno	The traditional oven used to cook agave *piñas*.
Jimador	The laborer who harvests agave.
Joven abocado	The same as *abocado*, unaged tequila to which coloring and flavoring has been added.
Madre	"Mother." Designates a mature agave plant from which *hijuelos* have been harvested.
Maguey	A Spanish term encompassing all varieties of agave.
Mezcal	A distilled drink made primarily in Oaxaca from various types of agave.
Mixto	Tequila produced using a mixture of agave sugars and other plant sugars.

Mosto	Must, the fermenting *aguamiel*.
Mosto muerto	The *aguamiel* after fermentation is completed.
NOM	*Norma Oficial Mexicana*. The official number assigned by the government to each tequila distillery; delineates which company made or bottled the tequila.
Ordinario	Liquid from the first distillation when making tequila.
Piña	The pineapple-shaped harvested agave plant.
Piloncillo	Unrefined sugar made from dried sugar cane juice used in production of *mixto* tequila.
Pipon	Tank, usually made of wood, used for storing tequila.
Pulque	A fermented, undistilled drink made from the sap of the agave plant.
Reposado	Tequila aged in wooden containers for at least two months but less than a year.
Tahona	The ancient traditional stone wheel used to crush and extract juice from cooked agave.

INDEX

THE TEQUILA TASTING FORM

TEQUILA					
DATE TASTED		**NOM**			

ATTACK					
INTENSITY	wimpy	light	full	strong	wow!
TACTILE	mellow/soft			pungent/burning	

COLOR					
	colorless	pale yellow	yellow	golden	gold/brown

AGAVE COMPLEXITY		
	sencillo	suave

AGAVE INTENSITY			
	light	moderate	macho	muy macho

AROMA	none	slight	moderate	high	¡ay caramba!
Earthy: ginseng/wet cement					
Fruity: lemon/citrus					
Floral: chamomile					
Spicy: white pepper					
Caramel: cream soda					
Smoky: oaky					
Volatile: acetone/overripe apple					
Other:					

SWEETNESS		
	low	sweet	syrupy

THE TEQUILA TASTING FORM
SIDE TWO

MOUTH FEEL			
	thin	medium	oily

FLAVOR	none	slight	moderate	high	¡ay caramba!
Agave					
Fruit/floral					
Spice/pepper					
Caramel					
Oak					
Smoky					
Acetone/overripe apple					
Other:					

FINISH				
SWEETNESS	none	low	medium	high
BITTERNESS	none	low	medium	high
DURATION OF FLAVOR	short	medium		long
FLAVOR				

ALCOHOL			
	tingly	hot	lip numbing

COMMENTS

THE TEQUILA TASTING FORM

TEQUILA					
DATE TASTED		NOM			

ATTACK					
INTENSITY	wimpy	light	full	strong	wow!
TACTILE	mellow/soft			pungent/burning	

COLOR					
	colorless	pale yellow	yellow	golden	gold/brown

AGAVE COMPLEXITY		
	sencillo	suave

AGAVE INTENSITY			
	light	moderate	macho	muy macho

AROMA	none	slight	moderate	high	¡ay caramba!
Earthy: ginseng/wet cement					
Fruity: lemon/citrus					
Floral: chamomile					
Spicy: white pepper					
Caramel: cream soda					
Smoky: oaky					
Volatile: acetone/overripe apple					
Other:					

SWEETNESS		
	low	sweet	syrupy

THE TEQUILA TASTING FORM
SIDE TWO

MOUTH FEEL	thin	medium	oily

FLAVOR	none	slight	moderate	high	¡ay caramba!
Agave					
Fruit/floral					
Spice/pepper					
Caramel					
Oak					
Smoky					
Acetone/overripe apple					
Other:					

FINISH

SWEETNESS	none	low	medium	high
BITTERNESS	none	low	medium	high

DURATION OF FLAVOR	short	medium	long

FLAVOR			

ALCOHOL	tingly	hot	lip numbing

COMMENTS

THE TEQUILA TASTING FORM

TEQUILA	
DATE TASTED	**NOM**

ATTACK					
INTENSITY	wimpy	light	full	strong	wow!
TACTILE	mellow/soft			pungent/burning	

COLOR					
	colorless	pale yellow	yellow	golden	gold/brown

AGAVE COMPLEXITY		
	sencillo	suave

AGAVE INTENSITY				
	light	moderate	macho	muy macho

AROMA	none	slight	moderate	high	¡ay caramba!
Earthy: ginseng/wet cement					
Fruity: lemon/citrus					
Floral: chamomile					
Spicy: white pepper					
Caramel: cream soda					
Smoky: oaky					
Volatile: acetone/overripe apple					
Other:					

SWEETNESS			
	low	sweet	syrupy

THE TEQUILA TASTING FORM
SIDE TWO

MOUTH FEEL			
	thin	medium	oily

FLAVOR	none	slight	moderate	high	¡ay caramba!
Agave					
Fruit/floral					
Spice/pepper					
Caramel					
Oak					
Smoky					
Acetone/overripe apple					
Other:					

FINISH				
SWEETNESS	none	low	medium	high
BITTERNESS	none	low	medium	high
DURATION OF FLAVOR	short	medium		long
FLAVOR				

ALCOHOL			
	tingly	hot	lip numbing

COMMENTS

Mail Orders

Send your check or money order to:

Wine Patrol Press
P.O. Box 228
Vineburg, CA 95487

Or fax (707) 996-5730

Please send ___ copies of *The Tequila Lover's Guide to Mexico.*

Name _____

Address _____

City_____ State ___ Zip _____

Price: The price of the book is $16.95 for the first copy, but only $13.95 for each additional copy. Buy several and give them to other tequila lovers.

Shipping: $3.00 for the first book, and $1.00 for each additional book in the same package.

Sales tax: Please add 7.5% for items shipped to a California address.

Amount enclosed _____

Also from Wine Patrol Press
Cold Surveillance: The Jake Lorenzo Wine Columns
by Jake Lorenzo

Cold Surveillance is the best book about wine that I've read in years.

Jerry Henry
WWL Radio, New Orleans

In the wonderful, but complex world of wine, there is nobody like Jake Lorenzo. Nobody. He is our Henry Miller, our Paul Gaugin, our Robin Williams.

Bob Sessions
Hanzell Vineyards

Ever outrageous, ever exhilarating, ever for freedom without distinction, ever for life at its most intense.

Gerald Asher
Gourmet Magazine

Pull up a chair, open a bottle, and enter Jake's world.
A bottle of wine will never be the same.

Even more from Wine Patrol Press

Making Wine at Home the Professional Way
with Lance Cutler

A unique, entertaining and remarkably educational video and workbook package that explains each step involved in the making of fine wine. Lance demonstrates every step from picking the grapes to crushing, pressing, fermenting, and bottling. His concept of demonstrating each process on a small, easy-to-understand home winemaker's scale, and then showing the same process at a larger commercial winery scale is truly inspired. The viewer learns what happens, why it happens, and how it is done.

If most "professional" winemakers watched this video, their wines would improve.

Jake Lorenzo
Practical Winery and Vineyards

While there are home winemaking books that offer excellent guidance, none create such a vivid portrayal as this combination video and workbook.

Jeff Morgan
The Wine Spectator

By combining hands-on "home" winemaking and professional winemaking, Lance has made winemaking really clear to people. Well done.

Gerald Asher
Gourmet Magazine

ORDER NOW!

Making Wine at Home the Professional Way
with Lance Cutler

Video only $29.95 (plus $3.00 shipping)

Workbook only $11.95 (plus $2.00 shipping)

Video/workbook package $35.95 (plus $3.00 shipping)

ORDER FORM

Send your check or money order to:

Wine Patrol Press
P.O. Box 228
Vineburg, Ca, 95487

Name _____

Address _____

City _____ State _____ Zip _____

Title	Price	Number of copies	Total
The Tequila Lovers Guide to Mexico	$16.95	_____	_____
Making Wine at Home the Professional Way			
(video)	$29.95	_____	_____
(workbook)	$11.95	_____	_____
(package)	$35.95	_____	_____
Cold Surveillance	$ 9.95	_____	_____
Shipping			_____
Tax			_____
Total			_____

Shipping: $3.00 for the first book or video, and $1.00 for each additional book or video in the same package.

Sales tax: Please add 7.5% for items shipped to a California address.

1998